Amid the Fall,
Dreaming of Eden

Amid the Fall, Dreaming of Eden

Du Bois, King, Malcolm X,
and Emancipatory Composition

Bradford T. Stull

Southern Illinois University Press
Carbondale and Edwardsville

Library of Congress Cataloging-in-Publication Data
Stull, Bradford T., 1961–
Amid the Fall, dreaming of Eden : Du Bois, King, Malcolm
X, and emancipatory composition / Bradford T. Stull.
    p. cm.
    Includes bibliographical references and index.
    1. Afro-Americans—Intellectual life—20th century.
2. Afro-Americans—Civil rights—History—20th century.
3. Rhetoric—Political aspects—United States—History—20th
century. 4. Political oratory—United States—History—20th
century. 5. Du Bois, W. E. B. (William Edward Burghardt),
1868–1963. 6. King, Martin Luther, Jr., 1929–1968. 7. X,
Malcolm, 1925–1965. 8. Racism—United States—Political
aspects. 9. Politics and literature—United States—History—
20th century. I. Title.
E185.61.S918 1999
305.896'073'00922—dc21   98-51923
ISBN 0-8093-2249-8 (cloth : alk. paper)   CIP

*For Elias and
Maggie, sweet
scents each*

Contents

Preface

As a religion major and a ministry student, I molted my faith in Jesus, even as I became more firmly aware of the profound injustices that, in part, constitute the world. This process was, I must add, no simple reduction of faith, no metonymic play. I was not replacing a boy's faith in Jesus with a commitment to social struggle, to justice.

My boyhood faith, after all, was profoundly shaped by the theo-political gospel stories I learned in Sunday school at the First Christian Church (Disciples of Christ) in Greeley, Colorado. Jesus, I came to know in my bones, was a Jewish provocateur deeply committed to the outcast. It was he, while preaching the love of God, who consorted with the marginal peoples of Galilean society. It was he, while condemning that era's equivalent of our own religious and social bourgeoisie, who upheld the Samaritan other as the great example of human-ness.

Thus, I suppose, it was only natural that I was shaken by the profundity of our contemporary social problems, that I would gravitate to a form of Christian religious practice deeply committed to addressing the "-isms" of the day, namely those arising from technology, the military, sex, class, and, above all, race. I thus trained to be a minister who could link the gospel to the rampant technologism that threatens the viability of the natural environment; a minister who could address, from the witness of the church, the problem of militarism, especially as it is manifest in the preparation for nuclear war; a minister who could bring the message of agape to bear in a world that continues to marginalize and oppress women; a minister who could help alleviate the suffering of poor Americans hurt by class conflict and class determinism; a minister, finally, who would help re-create the world so that elderly African American women would not have to end their lives in the squalor of public housing projects like the Robert Taylor Homes in Chicago and their grandchildren would not begin their lives with dozens of cockroaches as playmates.

However, I never did become that fiery, prophetic minister dedicated to peace and social justice.

I became, instead, a professor of English.

Acknowledgments

Amid the Fall, Dreaming of Eden has not one root but many. William A. Covino and David Jolliffe: the handful of bibliographic entries I wrote for their text on rhetoric served as the germinative work for this book. Indiana University East: its generous summer research grant provided me with three months of compositional freedom; its extraordinary library staff energized me with their passion for research and scholarship and their dedication to service. Stephen Webb, Patricia Bizzell, William A. Covino, Sharon Dean, and Paul Lizotte: each read portions of this book as it was being written and revised, and honestly cared. Tracy Sobol and John Gehner, my former and current editor at Southern Illinois University Press: Tracy saw this book's potential and patiently set it on its way; with professionalism John continued from where Tracy ended. The students in English Language–Development and Issues, at Rivier College: they participated in fecund discussions about cultural literacy and *Cultural Literacy*, discussions central to this project. Southern Illinois University Press readers: they chipped the edges, firmed the core. Michael Birkel: throughout the writing of this book, he served as a model Quaker scholar. Elias Stull Kim and Maggie Kim: together, they are the taproot.

**Amid the Fall,
Dreaming of Eden**

1 | Emancipatory Composition

Stated bluntly, immediately, with no appeal to narrative descriptions of oppression, of emancipation, of pain, of joy, here is the question that drives this book: What is the sociopolitical telos of composition studies? Or, put more simply, whom, what, does composition serve?

One might hold that oral and written discourse may or may not have political potential, may or may not address the quagmire of problems that Americans currently face. One might seek to teach clarity, organization, concision, what-have-you, as goods in and of themselves, ends to be achieved without particular reference to sociopolitical concerns. This, it seems, is the option chosen by theorists and practitioners such as E. D. Hirsch. While his *Cultural Literacy* firmly argues for the political ramifications of composition studies, his earlier book *The Philosophy of Composition* sees little, if any, interplay between composition and the polis. Any reference to the sociopolitical impact of composition is secondary to the "apolitical" norms of discourse.

Or, one might hold that most students should be taught to uphold the liberal, capitalist, democratic status quo. America, after all, offers a plethora of rights and goods unthinkable, perhaps even unachievable, in many countries; most students should be taught not to compose other, better sociopolitical orders but to sustain and strengthen the one in which they currently live. This is the option forcefully held by Richard Rorty in *Contingency, irony, and solidarity*. While he does allow for the presence of what he calls "strong poets," those few who can and should compose their own identities anew through reading and writing, speaking and listening, most people are to be taught to reproduce liberal democracy. The point of composition studies is not to challenge the social order but to maintain it.

Or, one might maintain that the current sociopolitical structure is wanting, in need of change. Rather than declare neutrality, rather than uphold, however fine it might be, the current ordering of the American experience, one might construct syllabi, reading lists, assignments, conferences and conference papers, e-mail, readers, and whatnot with an eye toward change, with the hope of improving the commonwealth, with the belief that the study of composition can, should, help set free the captives and give sight to the blind. Most forcefully and influentially elucidated by Paulo Freire in his famous *Pedagogy of the Oppressed*, this option has numerous contemporary American proponents, among them Ira Shor, Henry Giroux, and Donaldo Macedo.

This book rejects option one as foolhardy. No such thing as the neutral practice of composition exists. Even such minutiae as the comma splice have sociopolitical ramifications. British English tends to allow the commas splice; American English does not. Thus, to teach a group of college composition students to avoid, upon the pain of a lower grade, the comma splice, is to teach them to sustain, through the practice of discourse, a certain sociopolitical order, a certain way-of-being-in-the-world.

Option two, while truer to the inherent sociopolitical ramifications of the practice of composition, is also flawed: it is too fatalistic, too elitist. It is too fatalistic because it claims that liberal, capitalist democracy is the best that Americans can achieve. In contrast, America has yet to fulfill the utopian dreams embedded in its founding documents and dreams: that it is, in fact, a land of liberty and justice for all. Too, this option, at least as it is articulated by Rorty, is elitist: it would limit the full potential of composing to a privatized group. This claim is fraught with troubling questions, unanswered all: will the strong poets inevitably arise from a sociopolitically privileged class that emphasizes to its young the importance and potential of composition? Conversely, are children from sociopolitically disadvantaged households, households that tend not to emphasize the importance and potential of composition, left merely to an education that will prepare them to sustain the social order?

Bound by my own tripartite delineation, I claim option three as my own. Of course, I do not accept what my forebears have already articulated. Or, rather, I accept their articulations as helpful but limited. I too want to pursue questions like these: Can the study of composition serve the creation of a just commonwealth? If it can, how can it? What might emancipatory composition, a composition meant to set free the captives and give sight to the blind, be?

The short answer is this: emancipatory composition is radically theopolitical. A longer version? It is radically theopolitical, on one hand, because as it seeks to set free the captives and give sight to the blind, it roots itself in the foundational theological and political language of the American experience. It is radically theopolitical, on the other hand, because as it does so it calls into question this language and thus the American experience itself. Hence, it is at once conservative and extreme. Emancipatory composition would simultaneously dedicate itself to the study of the foundational vocabulary of the nation while embracing what Kenneth Burke calls "the comic attitude," an attitude that would allow it to subvert this vocabulary in order that its telos might be reached: the emancipation of the oppressed and thereby, as Martin Luther King Jr. would say, the oppressors. The task of this book is to make this answer even longer, to complicate the easy elucidation of the first sentence of this paragraph.

To do so, this book will proceed inductively, rooting itself in exemplary texts, examining the ways in which emancipatory composition has worked. I look, then, to those who compose not from a place of emancipated privilege but from a place in need of emancipation. Following Patricia Bizzell's lead, what I am calling "emancipatory composition" is best seen in "speakers and writers who are native to one of the non-dominant American cultures but who have also set themselves to master the dominant culture, in order to build rhetorical bridges to the members of this culture and effect social change" (5).

In particular, I attend to those who speak about the problem of race from the "dark side" of what W. E. B. Du Bois called the color line. This is not to suggest that other forms of oppression are not pressing—they are—but the problem of the color line is unique and fundamental. It is unique because no other oppressed group has been enslaved in America. It is fundamental because America, literally, was built on the institution of slavery. I hope that from the unique and fundamental nature of the problem of the color line, the work of emancipatory composition will gain great clarity.

I suggest, then, that the work of Du Bois and his heirs, Malcolm X and Martin Luther King Jr., provides fecund material for the elucidation of a theory of emancipatory composition. Discovered in their compositions are radical theopolitical practices, practices that draw on theological and political tropes of the American experience in order both to affirm and to challenge America, in order to support the emancipation of people bound by racism. These tropes are the Fall, the Orient, Africa, and Eden.

The exegesis of their work—the business of chapters 2 through 5— will necessarily lead to a reconsideration of a phrase simultaneously heralded and maligned: cultural literacy. The conclusion will suggest, albeit briefly, that E. D. Hirsch's phrase is not without merit. In short, Hirsch is correct to hold that there is a vocabulary that is central to the national experience, a vocabulary we would all do well to make a working part of our lives. However, Hirsch is incorrect to suggest that this vocabulary is not a tool of cultural and class oppression and emancipation. This book, through a reading of Du Bois, King, and Malcolm X, will demonstrate that there is a national vocabulary and that this vocabulary—how it is defined, used, abused— is crucial to the emancipation of human beings. Before I turn to these tasks, however, a number of preliminary questions must be answered, first among them this: why this book, anyway?

The Theoretical Tradition

Coming as it does in the wake of Paulo Freire's death, one must wonder if "emancipatory literacy," as Freire and his followers would call it, has not already been satisfactorily theorized, has not already been articulated as a counterweight to oppression. Needless to say, I think that fuller theoretical articulation is needed.

Before I turn to that discussion, however, two words of clarification are in order. First, this book centers around the word "composition" rather than literacy because it wants to draw attention to the following idea: Reading and writing—literacy—have been given far too privileged a place in American education to the detriment of listening and speaking. "Composition" indicates a state of intentionality, a process of study: one can compose a piece of writing just as one can compose an oral discourse. One can read a text just as one can listen. The current split between "composition" on one hand and "speech" on the other—prevalent in American colleges and universities—belies the reality of the communicative process. Most people live in written and oral worlds simultaneously, asked to perform competently as writers and speakers, readers and auditors. Consider any faculty meeting at any college: faculty members maneuver between written and oral texts constantly. Consider any business meeting where a junior executive communicates by speaking while referring to written text; she also expects her audience to listen and read.

So, too, consider briefly the compositional education of the three figures who are at the heart of this book. A detailed, comparative study of the educations of Du Bois, King, and Malcolm X would reveal much about the history of composition pedagogy and also speak to educators concerned about its future. Arnold Rampersand and Richard Lischer have already begun to explore the composition educations of Du Bois and King, respectively, and offer fine leads into this area of inquiry. Du Bois, as is well known, was raised in a New England town, apart from the vibrant rhetoric of the black church. He matriculated at Fisk, where he edited the school paper and developed a reputation for "excellence in oratory" (Rampersand 21). He took a second B.A. at Harvard, where he studied rhetoric with Barrett Wendell and Josiah Royce. Rampersand argues that Du Bois, under the tutelage of Wendell and Royce, learned classical rhetoric and that this is manifest in much of his professional work (36). As Lischer tells his readers, King studied a range of compositional models and practices: that of the black church in which he was raised, the intellectual, gentlemanly rhetoric of Morehouse College, the belles lettres and essay style of Crozier Theological Seminary (39–64).

Likewise, Malcolm X, in a famous section of the *Autobiography of Malcolm X*, discusses his own prison-based composition training, where he learned agonistic oratory in prison debates, studied the dictionary, read voluminously, and wrote copious letters to family members and, most importantly, to Elijah Muhammad. Further, as we

learn from Imam Benjamin Karim, Malcolm X, as a minister with the
Nation of Islam, came to organize a composition academy of sorts: it
emphasized public speaking in addition to history and other subjects
(10).

The second word of clarification is this: by "emancipation" this
book follows the lead provided by Schubert M. Ogden, a so-called
process theologian, which means that his theological work is indebted
to the philosophies of Alfred North Whitehead and Charles Hart-
shorne. Ogden, writing of the theological movement called "liberation theology," suggests that to work for emancipation

> is to labor for fundamental social and cultural change—the kind of
> structural or systematic change in the very order of our society and
> culture that is clearly necessary if each and every person is to be the
> active subject of his or her history instead of merely its passive object.
> (94)

That said, as it articulates a vision of emancipatory composition,
this book offers an alternative to theories of composition propagated
by the Right and Left alike. One such theory on the Right suggests
that composition training is intended to bring about desired socio-
economic/political ends in a time of shrinking resources, a collapsing
economy, and growing global economic competition. Identified by
Paulo Freire as "utilitarian" literacy, it is pushed in the industrial West
by businesses and the government and in the third world by the
United Nations Educational, Scientific, and Cultural Organization
(UNESCO) as a functional panacea for ills, both social and individual
(Freire and Macedo 146–47). It is perhaps not surprising that Barbara
Bush, as a representative of the Reagan-Bush administrations, once
exhorted the nation to "just say literacy."

At its worst, utilitarian literacy educates "functional literates" (Freire
and Macedo 146) like the one described by Jonathan Kozol. Benjamin, the functionally literate son of an old friend, was taught his
skill by the army. "One day he may have his chance to press the
button that releases that long, trim, slim, and slender instrument of
death that he so much resembles. Is this the kind of literacy we want?
Is this the best that Jeffersonian democracy can do?" (85–86). The
same must be asked of those workers who are taught to be function-

ally literate and take jobs in nuclear weapons factories, industries that
contribute to environmental pollution, corporations that readily aban-
don workers in one community in order to move to the third world
so that they may exploit inexpensive labor and lax environmental
standards.

Even the "height" of U.S. literacy, which Freire terms "academic"
(Freire and Macedo 145), is problematic. As Freire, Giroux, and others have argued, such literacy is chauvinistic and initiatory. As chauvinistic, it too often ignores the history of the underclasses and the
third world, thereby perpetuating an imperialistic, oppressive culture
that has reified itself with such terms as the New Israel and such policies as the Monroe Doctrine. As initiatory, it embeds within its students this chauvinism. Many college students, for instance, are ignorant about the division and reunification of Germany and about the
U.S. domination of native North Americans and Latin Americans.

To counter these theories of literacy, Freire, Giroux, Ira Shor, and
other left-wing educators propose that concerned teachers who, as
Giroux puts it, want to help establish "radical" democracy (*Teachers*
173) must opt for a practice and theory of "emancipatory literacy."
This is the theory to which the idea of "emancipatory composition" is
the most indebted; this theory is also one that suffers from two problematic tendencies: "emancipatory literacy" tends to speak monologically, and it tends to forget the conservative nature of radicalism.

As Giroux understands it, a theory of emancipatory literacy

> points to the need to develop an alternative discourse and critical
> reading of how ideology, culture, and power work within late capital-
> ist societies to limit, disorganize, and marginalize the more critical
> and radical everyday experiences and common-sense perceptions of
> individuals. (*Schooling* 152)

Unlike the utilitarian and academic theories, emancipatory literacy is
concerned to locate words within history and power relations, to locate words within the discourse from which they arise and to which
they return.

The problem is that the other theories of literacy are thoroughly
dominant and that emancipatory literacy is grossly undertheorized
(Giroux, *Schooling* 148–50); Giroux himself has only tentatively be-

gun to provide a theoretical foundation for it. Such theorizing is necessary because all practice is guided by a philosophy of some sort. In order to control their practice, composition theorists must make their philosophies explicit and appropriate. If emancipatory composition is ever to become the way in which we teach ourselves to read and write, to speak and listen, it must be justified theoretically.

Both Freire and Giroux, as they have attempted to justify emancipatory literacy, point to the "dangerous memory" of oppressed and suffering peoples, both living and dead. Freire, for instance, claims that emancipatory literacy is "grounded in a critical reflection on the cultural capital of the oppressed" (Freire and Macedo 157); traditional approaches to literacy, in contrast, celebrate scientific method and rigor, reducing history "to a footnote" (Freire and Macedo 145). This appeal to the history of the oppressed is crucial because it "leads at once to the recognition of dehumanization, not only as an ontological possibility but as an historical reality. And as man perceives the extent of dehumanization, he asks himself if humanization is a viable possibility" (Freire, *Pedagogy* 27). Though this remembrance of the suffering of the oppressed is central to Freire's work, and for good reason, it is essentially undeveloped. Giroux, in his *Schooling and the Struggle for Public Life*, attempts to develop it more fully but finally presumes its theoretical explication.

Central to his book are the claims that "America is becoming a land without memory" (*Schooling* 80) and that the dominant ideology wishes it to be so in order to extinguish discordant and suffering voices that would necessarily disrupt the status quo. In order to counter this, Giroux suggests that radical educators should turn to liberation theology, which would have us reclaim the dangerous memory of the oppressed and thereby rupture the monological voice that attempts to silence it (93). As Giroux argues, once we recall the narrative memories of suffering people, "truth" is shown to be the outcome of power struggles that cannot be abstracted from networks of power and control.

As a theoretical justification for emancipatory composition, this retrieval of the dangerous memory of the suffering and oppressed human subject, this privileging of the poor, is promising. For instance, "Just Say No," the Reagan-era anti-drug spell, muffles an urban African American subculture pervaded by drug problems largely created by an oppressive social situation rooted in slavery. "Just Say No" would have one believe that one only needs to chant the incantation in order to overcome drug addiction.

In fact, the situation is much more complex. One must locate Reagan's drug discourse in the larger history and power systems that generated it. Once one is able to discern this complexity, the teaching of emancipatory composition becomes theoretically justified simply because one hears the rumblings of the oppressed voices underlying all discourse. In order to be true to the historical and power dimensions of language, schools must teach emancipatory composition. Any other act is a suppression of oppressed subjects on which history is built. If one is at all moved by the suffering of peasants in Latin America, Jews in Auschwitz, migrant workers here in the United States, the very environment that is rapidly being destroyed, one must, at the very least, consider helping the oppressed to find their voices. These voices can be heard only when their participation in our discourse is recognized and their subjecthood affirmed.

However, it is in this affirmation of subjecthood that emancipatory literacy tends both to speak monologically and to forget the radical possibilities of conservatism. While Giroux speaks of the singular "oppressed," of the singular "poor," there is no such singular. As the ensuing chapters will show, the "oppressed" offer heterogeneous interpretations of their situations. Giroux seems to seek "an alternative discourse," but this dream of the singular is an illusion.

Giroux also too easily denies the possibility of the extreme nature of the conservative elements of American culture. This book affirms the extreme possibilities of conservative communal experiences, like the Fourth of July and the document that gave rise to this holiday. While the Fourth of July has degenerated into a day of barbecues and senseless fireworks released by teenagers, it speaks of the insatiable desire for freedom at the heart of the American experience.

Consider, briefly, King's remarkable "I Have a Dream" text. Lucy Anne McCandish Keele argues that

> although King was a critic of the society and its processes, his rhetoric clearly indicates that he endeavored to justify the civil rights move-

ment in terms of the best inherent in the society. He did not advocate another system, but rather identified the civil rights struggle with . . . the "American Dream." (187)

At one level, Keele is quite correct. "I Have a Dream" does elucidate the utopian impulse at the heart of the American tradition, and it does draw on the country's rhetorical heritage in order to elucidate this utopia. However, Keele misses a key dimension of King's text, a dimension that ultimately radicalizes King. While an idea of utopia is at the heart of the American tradition, the utopia about which King speaks is broader and richer than what American society has hitherto been able to imagine. King speaks of communitarianism, a word that represents a society where all social divisions, including the color line, have been overcome. King releases the oppressed other hidden in the American utopian desire, thus revealing a model compositional practice.

Composition from the Color Line

Certainly, emancipatory composition is concerned to address a host of issues and problems, not just the problem of race. However, the issue of race is particularly generative for emancipatory composition for three reasons. First, it is, arguably, the problem of the twentieth century, as Du Bois has suggested. Second, composition is central to the problem of race; thus, the problem of race sheds penetrating light on the problem of emancipatory composition. Third, three exemplars of the civil rights movement—Du Bois, King, and Malcolm X— are likewise exemplars of emancipatory composition, and thus their work proves to be fecund territory for a theory of emancipatory composition.

Many folk are tempted to think that the problem of race is a historic artifact, something that once existed in American history. Consider, for instance, a young lawyer with a powerful Rocky Mountain region firm. She holds firmly, even dearly, to the belief that there is no race problem, only a problem of individual initiative. She sees not groups bound by the history of conflict and antagonism but individuals limited only by their own laziness.

Cornel West, the great contemporary academic theorist and grass-roots activist, tells a different story, or rather stories, in the preface of *Race Matters*. One: Dressed immaculately as usual in his standard three-piece suit, West waited on a New York City street corner for a taxicab to take him to an appointment with a photographer. Nine cabs refused him, an African American academic; the tenth refused him and picked up a well-dressed woman of European descent standing next to him. Two: While driving to Williams College in Williamstown, Massachusetts, to teach religion, he was stopped by a police officer, charged with trafficking cocaine, and called a "nigger." In both cases, the point is clear. West was viewed not as an individual but as a member of a group. The police officer and cab drivers were on one side of the line, and West, with all "niggers," was on the other.

One may grant that the cabbie's fear and the policeman's suspicion were not totally irrational. After all, recent reports indicate that "one in three black males between the ages of 20 and 29 is in prison, on parole, or on probation" (Ford 1). Nonetheless, most African American males are not on the "wrong side of the law." They are stereotyped as such and, as a result, suffer as a group.

The south side of Chicago only confirms the universality of West's encounters. Hyde Park—the neighborhood of the University of Chicago—is separated from surrounding neighborhoods, all African American, by numerous lines: one-way streets, cul-de-sacs, vacant lots, among them. Through the use of these various strategies, the neighborhood effectively has constructed a physical boundary that separated affluent, educated, multicultural Hyde Park from some of the most destitute neighborhoods in the United States. One might say that Hyde Park excludes "the poor" rather than African Americans. This is true enough, keeping in mind that, on Chicago's south side, race and class are inseparable. On the whole, the poor are African Americans. So too, as Brent Staples reminds us, Hyde Park is not without its racial suspicions. As an African American University of Chicago graduate student, he was the cause of fear and suspicion as he walked the streets of his own neighborhood.

Less obvious, but perhaps even more powerful, is the psychic line that lies between the typical Hyde Parker and other citizens of the south side. One can, at most any time of day or night, encounter

Hyde Parker discourse, which was, for all intents and purposes, University of Chicago discourse: game theory, Kant, calcium inhibitors, feminist hermeneutics. It is, perhaps, needless to say that people living in the housing projects at 40th Street and Lake Park, merely eighteen blocks away from the heart of Hyde Park, seven blocks from its outskirts, have different things on their minds.

Lest one think that the color line is endemic only to the great metropolitan areas like New York and Chicago, consider a small midwestern town, proud of its friendliness, its traditional values. Its country club, comprising the town's power elite, attempted to persuade a local university away from hiring an African American chancellor. The reason? The chancellorship included a membership at the club and, well, no African American had ever been a member.

Return to Hyde Park, Chicago. As was suggested above, the neighborhood is separated from its south-side partners by physical and linguistic lines. Physically, there are one-way streets, cul-de-sacs, and dead-ends. Linguistically, there is game theory, Kant, calcium inhibitors, feminist hermeneutics, and the like. The two aspects of the line do, certainly, overlap. The physical barriers allow for the leisurely discussion of game theory on 57th Street; the more people enjoy leisurely discussing game theory on 57th Street, the more they will support physical barriers that allow them to do so. However, the physical and linguistic barriers are not the same. A series of vacant lots that separate somatically an affluent, multiracial community from a poor, African American community is not the same thing as discourse that separates these communities psychically.

The example of Hyde Park discourse is, perhaps, innocuous. While Kantian discourse among a group of young men and women standing at the corner of 57th Street and Kenwood Avenue is, in the big picture, implicated in the color line, its connection is not immediately obvious. Thus, the "rhetorical effect" of this example, without detailed explication, is not as strong as it might be. Let this example float and consider others in an attempt to build a range of scenes.

The history of the interpretation of the Constitution of the United States of America can be read as a history of the interpretation of the discourse of the color line. *Brown v. Board of Education of Topeka* (1954) was, after all, an interpretive struggle over constitutional words and the ways in which these words determined the lives of people of color in America.

"Nigger," as Cornel West reminds his readers, is a crude but powerful example of the discourse of the color line. The police officer who mistakenly accused him of being a cocaine trafficker demarcated his world from West's not simply by the somatic act of flashing his lights, of stopping him on the road, of showing a badge. The officer's discourse announced the manifest presence of the line.

Finally, consider two episodes in the life of Malcolm X. The first is about a history class he took as a middle-schooler. He remembers the time when the class

> came to the . . . section on Negro history. It was exactly one paragraph long. Mr. Williams laughed through it practically in a single breath, reading aloud how the Negroes had been slaves and then were freed, and how they were usually lazy and dumb and shiftless. He added, I remember, an anthropological footnote on his own, telling us between laughs how Negroes' feet were "so big that when they walk, they don't leave tracks, they leave a hole in the ground." (*Autobiography* 29)

The discourse of the history book and the teacher, which combined to form the discourse of Malcolm X's history class, drew the color line clearly. For the book, African Americans deserved only slight mention, and derogatory mention at that. For the teacher, the book needed elaboration, a joke to drive home the point and even to contradict emancipation itself. The Negroes of the joke are not human. The joke's implicit message is, perhaps, that the emancipation was a mistake. After all, why should one provide human freedom to those who are not human?

This entry into the discourse of the color line seems to have had little immediate impact on Malcolm X. Despite the history book's narrative, he continued to like the subject; despite the teacher's language, he continued to like school. Only later did the discourse of the color line drive Malcolm X "away from white people," as he put it (*Autobiography* 36–37).

Asked by a teacher what he would be when he grew up, Malcolm said that he would be a lawyer. The teacher suggested, in a reasonable tone, that Malcolm X needed to be realistic: he was, after all, a "nigger." The teacher told Malcolm X to choose a manual trade, like carpentry, rather than the law as means by which to live. The nouns that the teacher used, and the sociopolitical power they represent, devastated Malcolm X. He found himself marked by the vocabulary of a racist society, cast to one side of the line. It is not unimportant to note that the teacher was not merely attempting to persuade Malcolm X to become a manual laborer. He was attempting to dissuade Malcolm X from becoming a lawyer, a member of a professional caste that concerns itself with the discourse that controls society legally. The teacher's racism drove Malcolm X away from a level of discourse that would have provided him entry into the legal power of American society.

Du Bois, King, Malcolm X

If the compositional intricacy of the color line is an excellent place, albeit not the only place, to discover the outlines of emancipatory composition, the compositional masterworks of Du Bois, King, and Malcolm X are themselves rich with possibility. These three are among the most important rhetoricians of the twentieth century. Each shaped social movements: Du Bois, the National Association for the Advancement of Colored People (NAACP) and the civil rights movement; King, the civil rights and anti-war movements; Malcolm X, the separatist movement. Each contributed mightily to the discourse that would challenge the color line. This is true even of Malcolm X, both in his separatist, pre-Mecca days and in his post-Mecca, globe-embracing period. Separatism, properly understood, is a movement dedicated to the line's erasure just as much as integrationism is. The line indicates the presence of a dominated people oppressed by a dominator. Separatism would erase the line by totally demarcating the societies, allowing each to flourish without the other. There would be no line because the people involved would no longer share the same space.

In my attempt to read Du Bois, King, and Malcolm X as models for emancipatory composition, I focus, in the case of King and Malcolm X, on the range of their published work. For King, I draw on *A Testament of Hope*, a collection of his significant sermons, speeches, essays, and interviews. It includes, as well, excerpts from his books. For Malcolm X, I draw on the various collections of his speeches and interviews.

In the case of Du Bois, I focus on his writings published in the *Crisis*, the official periodical of the NAACP. Du Bois founded the *Crisis* and served as its editor for over twenty years, effectively shaping it as a powerful medium of public discourse on the color line. While Du Bois was an extraordinarily prolific writer, his pieces in the *Crisis* offer special insight into public rhetoric, as many students of Du Bois recognize (for example, Marable, Rampersand, Rudwick, Arndt, De Marco, Taylor, and Kimbrough). This book focuses on the *Crisis* writings for three reasons. First, as Arndt (and others) suggest, the *Crisis* "must be considered one of the most important organs of protest ever published in the United States" (24). Second, the *Crisis* represents Du Bois at his best. Broderick argues that "most of [Du Bois's] best writing appeared in his monthly editorials in which he clothed his facts with wit, paradox, indignation, and a call to arms" (156). The same can be said of all his work that appeared in the *Crisis*, not just the editorials. Third, the *Crisis*, and thus Du Bois's writing in it, had an extraordinary appeal. By the end of World War I, the magazine's circulation peaked at one hundred thousand. Throughout the 1920s, it maintained a base of sixty-five to seventy-five thousand subscribers (Arndt 28). Du Bois's work in the *Crisis* is mass composition, achieving a level of publicness that his sociological work and novels never reached.

In Du Bois, King, and Malcolm X, one finds the germinating seeds of emancipatory composition that is at once radical and theopolitical. Without doubt, this book's treatment of Du Bois, King, and Malcolm X might be met with skepticism. Aren't, common wisdom suggests, these three about social action, truth, justice, the liberation of their people? What have they to do with composition?

Imagine the Malcolm X who has, by all accounts, become a cultural icon that spans African American and Caucasian communities. One sees "X" caps and shirts, goatees, and "Malcolm X glasses" on Caucasian youth as readily as one sees them on African American youth; the *Autobiography* has become standard reading on many campuses;[1] Spike Lee's film adaptation of the *Autobiography* played well with Caucasian audiences. This Malcolm X who spans cultural contexts is not a figure of nuanced compositional analysis, not a figure who incites one to study with meticulous intensity the movement of words. He is the firebrand, the mythical white-hater, the man who posed by a window, rifle in arms, ready to change society "by any means necessary." Michael Dyson's tale about how his Brown University college students, especially the African American men, received Malcolm X makes this point. These young men were angry and wanted a certain sort of Malcolm X that they could claim for themselves; they were not afraid to reject defiantly other claims that other students, and Dyson himself, made for Malcolm X.

This book means to reaffirm what Dyson calls Malcolm X's "cultural renaissance" but means to recenter it by focusing on his composition. This is hardly the stuff of romance, of symbolic images meant to last a lifetime. Offered is not the angry, bombastic Minister Malcolm X delivering the "saucy put-down" (Dyson 85), not the white-robed Malcolm X speaking globally about the brotherhood of all people. Offered is not the thunderous King/Moses preaching to the multitudes at the reflecting pool, not the tender, pacifist King calming the threatening crowd after his home was bombed. Offered is not the dapper, double-Ph.D. Du Bois confabbing with the literary elite in New York, not the defiant, visionary Du Bois dying in Ghanaian exile. Offered, instead, is the Malcolm X of a compositionist, the King of an English professor, the Du Bois of a reader and writer. While this may never convince the newly politically aware MTV to feature this book, the compositions of Du Bois, King, and Malcolm X are, finally, among their most important contributions to American culture in general and to theories of composition in particular.

This aspect of their personas is, of course, difficult for the American culture industry to sell. Do people want to purchase a T-shirt of a Malcolm X, humbled by the realization that he lacked linguistic facility, reading the dictionary in prison? Do people want to purchase a T-shirt of Du Bois celebrating his enormous erudition, hard-earned at Fisk and Harvard? Do people want to purchase a T-shirt of King graduating from college? from seminary? from graduate school? Does the culture industry really want the public to consider, seriously, the liberative power one takes on when one takes on composition, when one takes on the force found in, say, Malcolm X's painful struggle in prison to find his public voice?

What if, for instance, the students in the undergraduate class at Indiana University East who read Malcolm X's *Autobiography* were more than fascinated (as they were) with the book? What if these rural women, who had had little experience with African American life and little knowledge of the problems with which urban folk struggle, had taken to heart Malcolm X's emancipatory composition, had become transformed by his call for a global, interracial movement against white capitalist, colonial and neocolonial oppression? The culture industry, finally, does not sell Malcolm X as a radical composer, as one who, like Du Bois and King, calls into question the social structure that allows things like the American culture industry to exist.

Theopolitical Tropes

While there are many ways into the emancipatory compositions of Du Bois, King, and Malcolm X, their work is especially powerful when considered in relation to four theopolitical tropes: the Fall, the Orient, Africa, and Eden.

A helpful way to think about the play of these tropes in the works of Du Bois, King, and Malcolm X is to place them within the tradition of "commonplaces" (or *koinoi topoi*). While commonplaces are an integral part of the history of education in the West, they have been largely discredited in the modern era because the point of education "has been increasingly to communicate a distinct, novel worldview and not to transmit conventional, accepted wisdom" (Covino and Jolliffe 40). However, this is precisely the point of emancipatory composition: to take the conventional and make it unconventional.

Another way to think about these tropes, and others like them, is through the work of Celeste Michelle Condit and John Louis Lucaites, in particular their term "ideograph." They write that

> an ideograph is a culturally biased, abstract word or phrase, drawn from ordinary language, which serves as a constitutional value for a historically situated collectivity. Ideographs represent in condensed form the normative, collective commitments of the members of the public and they typically appear in public argumentation as the necessary motivations or justifications for action performed in the name of the public. (xii–xiii)

Condit and Lucaites also emphasize that these ideographs are flexible and capable of handling many meanings. For them, for instance, "equality" is a negotiable term: many communities share it, but each deals with it a bit differently.

So too it is possible to use commonplaces to create novel worldviews and to disturb traditional worldviews. This is one of the points made by Condit and Lucaites: "equality" is used to invent and structure countercompositions. King's use of phrases from the Bible, for instance, does confirm the so-called Judeo-Christian heritage. However, King also disturbs it, employing these commonplaces/ideographs to envision an egalitarian society that would replace a society based on race, class, and gender distinctions.

The four central tropes of this book—the Fall, the Orient, Africa, and Eden—are sociopolitical and religious words that have been, and continue to be, constitutive of the American experience. Thus, this book places itself in the middle of an ongoing struggle in American compositional strategy. If American discourse is nothing else, it is an attempt to weave sociopolitical and religious language into a seamless garment that would clothe us. This is true of both the Right and the Left. Consider, for instance, this quotation from presidential candidate Ronald Reagan:

> Over the last two or three decades, the federal government seems to have forgotten both that old-time religion and that old-time Constitution. We have God's promise that if we turn to him and ask his help we shall have it. With this help we can still become that shining city upon a hill.[2] (Handy 206–7)

So too the Left weaves together the sociopolitical and the religious. An example of this is a document produced by an ecumenical group of religious leaders that tries to justify the act of religious institutions providing sanctuary to Salvadoran and Guatemalan refugees. This group appeals both to the Book of Exodus—" 'give shelter to the stranger among you' "—and to the history and laws of the United States:

> Our nation has accepted to provide asylum or refuge to persons who cannot return to their country of origin because of fear of persecution for reasons of race, religion, nationality, or membership in a particular social group of political opinion. (Golden and McConnell 204)

If religious words in general are an integral part of American discourse, "Fall of Man" and "Eden" are particularly important. Our "Pilgrim fathers" (to use another trope central to the American experience) based their mission to the New World on the interplay of these words: America was to be the New Israel, an Edenic construction that would overcome Adam's curse. The Orient and Africa also have an important position in American discourse, serving as sociopolitical others against which Americans often justify their own lives and judge their own actions. For example, the web of associations in which the word "Africa" existed (and does exist) helped justify slavery. The least malignant version ran something like this: it was the "dark continent," not yet open to the light of the New Israel; thus its inhabitants were necessarily subject to the redemption that paternal slavery would offer them. The most malignant version, it hardly needs be said, saw the "dark continent" as the home of evil creatures who needed to be subdued by the chosen ones.

The compositions of Du Bois, King, and Malcolm X are woven with the webs of these words in order to establish a place for themselves in the American tradition and in order to challenge it extremely. When Du Bois, for instance, speaks of Africa, he immediately connects with a web of associations that his audiences will have relative to this word. Thus, he and they become part of the same moment, the same history. However, Du Bois also manipulates this word so as to disrupt the American heritage. It becomes, for him, the sociopolitical/religious word that counters the word "America." Africa, for Du Bois, becomes the preferable other. It does not simply serve as an analogical corrective, used to make statements like "Let's look to Africa to see how we can improve America." Rather, Africa becomes the word of choice, the representative of a better place to be.

Chapters 2, 3, 4, and 5 will explore the play of the Fall, the Orient, Africa, and Eden, respectively. This is a deliberately chosen pattern. First, it weaves together the sociopolitical and religious words in order to remind readers that they cannot be composed separately. One cannot compose the dreams about Eden in Malcolm X, for instance, without composing Africa. Second, Du Bois, King, and Malcolm X all presume fallenness: it is the given condition out of which they work, from which they look to Asia, to Africa, to Eden, seeking, always, a way to compose America by composing the vocabulary central to the republic. The conclusion will, albeit briefly, connect this discussion of emancipatory composition to a concept composition theorists on the Left have too easily dismissed: cultural literacy.

2 | The Fall

> We have not developed the language by which to
> recognize the extent or the implications of the division.
>
> —Wendell Berry, *The Hidden Wound*

"The Fall," as a trope, alludes to the story of Adam and Eve, to that narrative double moment: humankind expelled from peace and union with all that is, humankind thrown into a world of violence and division. To know this phrase is to be able to begin to function maturely in the American republic, which is prerequisite for emancipatory composition. The Fall deeply informs American discourse in general and American discourse about the color line in particular.

Certainly, one must immediately ask this question: What does it mean to know the Fall? Or, phrased differently, more pointedly, what does the Fall mean? To what does it allude?

The most immediate association is with the Book of Genesis. In Eden, Adam and Eve walk naked with the Lord God and all the animals of the earth, sharing the garden in blissful harmony. With the bite of the fruit from the one tree made taboo, however, Adam and Eve deliver themselves into the post-Edenic world. Here, the Bible tells its readers, Adam and Eve are immediately condemned to interspecies strife (3:15), painful childbirth and gender hierarchy (3:16), hard labor (3:17–18), and death (3:19). A host of other events follow quickly upon the curse: Cain kills Abel; new races of humans that are divided from each other, and God, arise; God floods Noah's world; new races of humans attempt to build the Tower of Babel and are crushed, divided linguistically by a jealous God.

Thus, one could legitimately approach the Fall biblically. Certainly, many Americans encounter the Fall this way through the sermons, liturgies, and prayers of their churches and synagogues. These institutions promote a literacy in which the Fall is an important element. One cannot fully practice Christianity, for example, without having an understanding of the Fall and how it relates to the redemptive work of that second Adam, Jesus Christ.

Building on this religious approach to the Fall, one could follow the lead of an American theologian like the great Protestant Reinhold Niebuhr. He finds that the Fall is involved in a web of associations that speaks to the crises of the twentieth century (particularly those of the period between World War I and World War II). In order to combat what he calls error-plagued "alternatives to prophetic religion," he offers a reading of "the myth of the Fall" that reveals a peculiar combination of "profound pessimism" (because evil is the product of human responsibility) and "ultimate optimism" (because God is still present, thus offering the hope that good will triumph over evil). In order to reach and explore what the Fall reveals, Niebuhr delves into a wide-ranging, allusive web of words and phrases, among them "Hebrew mythology," Calvin and Luther, Albert Schweitzer, St. Paul, Marxism, Buddhism, Stoicism, Roman imperialism, the French Revolution, "Augustinian Christianity," Henri Bergson, and Freudian psychology (39–61).

The Fall is also a part of classic and contemporary literature. Turn to Milton, biblical poet/theologian that he was. Milton's great work *Paradise Lost* is, of course, a meditation on the heavenly and earthly intrigue that led to the expulsion from the garden. Milton, needless to say, is one of the giants of Anglo-American culture; *Paradise Lost* is taught in every American college, each year introducing new students to the Fall and the web of associations it involves. For these students who read Milton, the web of the Fall becomes more complex. The world into which Milton brings them—Satan, angels, the Beloved Son, heavenly battles—only complicates the Fall for them, making the web denser, thicker.

One needs to know the Fall in order to read not only Milton but also many contemporary writers. The American poet Mary Fell, for example, plays with the Fall in her poem "The Triangle Fire," which states that God granted "eternal toiling / on the workday side" (3). The opening of Fell's poem actually weaves together the first Genesis creation story and the Fall into a pastiche that addresses a tragedy born of the industrial order. The "split," at one level, alludes to the creation story, in which God created for six days and rested on the seventh. It also alludes to the Fall. The word "toil" takes the reader into the post-Edenic world where Adam is cursed to work with sweat and hardship.

Fell's poem is also instructive because it reveals the fully allusive nature of words. The poem never once mentions "Eden," never once mentions the Fall. It simply speaks of "God," "Sabbath," and "toil," letting the mind of the reader play with the web of connections these words reveal. Fell, in fact, need not say the Fall; the words "work" and "toil" metonymically bring one to the post-Edenic curse where Adam and Eve are consigned to hardship and pain.

The Fall does not belong only to institutional religious life, to theology, to literature. It permeates American culture. For instance, a national business alludes to it in order to market a product; its "all-natural" soft drink manufactured in and marketed from Vermont is named "After the Fall."

Consider, as well, a contemporary American effort—the Hollywood film *Legends of the Fall*. While this movie is certainly not an artistic masterpiece, it well demonstrates the pervasiveness of the Fall in American culture. The title, obviously, is the initial indication of the film's connection with the Fall, and the movie itself bears out the title. The opening scene depicts the American cavalry, led by a conscientious colonel, escorting a group of indigenous peoples out of their ancestral lands. The colonel is disgusted with the push westward and what it means for the natives. He leaves the cavalry and retreats to the Montana wilderness, creating an Edenic ranch where European Americans and indigenous people alike are welcome. Yet paradise is not complete. In one memorable scene, the audience learns that the colonel's best friend is a Cheyenne Indian who can speak English but refuses to do so; he protests the European American conquest by refusing its language. Thus, the film reveals one of the fundamental facts of the American experience. America's push west entailed both social dislocation and the imposition of language upon a conquered people. The push west manifests the Fall: people divided, violence used to further the division.

The compositional practices of church, synagogue, professional theology, literature, and other aspects of American culture inform this chapter because they help to define the Fall in the American context. However, the primary lead into the Fall is provided by Kenneth Burke, who has elucidated three pertinent aspects: violence, property division, and Babel.[1]

The first two aspects are revealed most concisely in a series of questions Burke asks while wondering whether humans must return to Eden in order to resolve the violence and division of the Fall:

> Where are we then? Are we proposing that men cannot resolve their local fights over property until they have undergone the most radical revolution of all, a return to their source? Are we saying that because the warlike divisiveness over property is inherent in our very nature, such mythic design justifies the *status quo* or can properly serve as an argument for the "inevitability" of some particular war? (*Rhetoric* 140)

As Burke himself says soon after this passage, he thinks that the answer is no. We don't have to return to Eden in order to stop the violent acquisition and defense of property. Nonetheless, he finds in the Fall an apt description of our problem. The state to which human beings were relegated upon expulsion from Eden is the state in which humans find themselves now, a state of violent conflict over property.

So too, and this is the primary dimension of the Fall as Burke understands it, humans are marked by "the communicative disorder that goes with the building of the . . . Tower of Babel" (139). Eden implies unity in language as well as property. With the Fall, then, also comes communicative divisions marked by violence. Humans are caught in a terrible situation. They are divided by language and property, caught in cycles of violence. While divisions may be reordered or even briefly overcome, they are inevitable, as is the violence that accompanies both the maintenance and reordering of these divisions.

Burke's interpretation of the Fall cautions one to remember, even foreground, the interrelatedness of composition and violence. The divisions that humans suffer within the Fall are not simply linguistic, though they are that. The divisions are also marked by blood and beaten bodies. Any sensible reading of the establishment of modern nations, and the attendant establishment of modern national languages, reminds us that "national unity" is had by the oppression of the other, be it the Scots and the Irish in the case of Great Britain or African slaves and the indigenous peoples of what is now the United States in the case of the United States. To focus on the "Babelish" nature of the contemporary American republic is to focus, as well, on violence. America, after all, is built, in part, on Africans enslaved to American national culture and language.

Du Bois's, King's, and Malcolm X's work with the Fall occurs without specific use of the term itself. Nonetheless, their works are rife with the Burkeian elements of the Fall: violence, socioeconomic division, and Babel. One cannot fully understand their work without knowing the Fall, and one cannot look to them as exemplars of emancipatory composition without coming to realize that a central characteristic of emancipatory composition is a commitment to the Fall, which is to say a commitment to composition that addresses violence, socioeconomic division, Babel.

Babel

From the vantage of emancipatory composition, Babel names communicative disorder. Yet, communicative disorder necessarily contains within itself the notion of order, just as communicative order necessarily contains within itself the notion of disorder. Babel points both to the desire for a true, unified language that can "speak to God" and to the impossibility of fulfilling that desire.

Du Bois, King, and Malcolm X, each in his own way, acknowledge both sides of Babel: the jangling diversity of language and the desire for unity in order to create a better social order. Nowhere in the work of the three does the doubleness of Babel manifest itself more fully than in Malcolm X's autobiography. There, Malcolm X powerfully reveals the bind. Reflecting on his prison education, he tells his readers that

> I became increasingly frustrated at not being able to express what I wanted to convey in letters that I wrote, especially those to Mr. Elijah Muhammad. In the street, I had been the most articulate hustler out there—I had commanded attention when I said something. But now, trying to write simple English, I not only wasn't articulate, I wasn't

even functional. How would I sound writing in slang, the way I would *say* it, something such as "Look, daddy, let me pull your coat about a cat, Elijah Mu–hammad." (171)

Malcolm X was removed from the streets of Harlem and Boston—and the ghetto discourse community in which he operated as a criminal—only to confront the discordant jangle of voices that is one aspect of Babel. As a hustler, Malcolm X was a self-acknowledged master of the only language necessary for survival in the hustler's world. He did not know other English dialects; for him, other English dialects were unimportant.[2]

In prison, however, once he began to explore the possibilities of the Nation of Islam, Malcolm X ran into the existence of another dialect, a dialect that was, at first, closed to him—so-called Standard American English (SAE). In fact, the dialect was more than that: it was, on its surface, another language. He claims that his early attempts to read were frustrated by this language barrier: the books "might as well have been in Chinese" (171).

The pull of SAE for Malcolm X was its "universality." "Universality" is in quotation marks because of the problematic nature of this phrase. SAE has achieved its status through historical accident, the rise of mass print media, and national schooling. Without doubt, nonstandard dialects do need to be taken seriously, for a variety of reasons. SAE should not simply be assumed as the natural, superior linguistic order. Yet, as Malcolm X, master of street slang might suggest, nonstandard dialects aren't good enough when one seeks to participate in the struggle of peoples outside a particular dialect community. Malcolm X's own street dialect, marked by such diction as "let me pull your coat about a cat," is powerful, beautifully poetic. But, he assures his readers, it is limited in communicative scope: most English speakers/writers/listeners/readers (and this included African Americans who were not taught this particular dialect) simply wouldn't know what it meant.

A perfect example of the Babel in which Malcolm X found himself arose years after he was assassinated, in a first-year college composition class I taught during the fall of 1994. The class was composed of twenty-four students: twenty-three European American men and women and one African American woman. As a way to delve into the problematic of dialects (including SAE), the students considered Malcolm X's sentence from the quotation above: "Look, daddy, let me pull your coat about a cat, Elijah Muhammad."

Not surprisingly, none of the twenty-three European Americans, including one who had a fairly sophisticated understanding of the play of language, understood it. They met it, as people often do when faced with their own inability to understand, with nervous laughter. In frustration, the African American woman explained it to them: "Let me tell you about a man, Elijah Muhammad."

The African American woman knew that language in American society is discordant and that she had to learn the more "universal" SAE in order to become validated by the SAE-dominated system. Dialect though it is, SAE is the "universal" dialect. In contrast, the European American students had never had to face Babel quite this baldly before; they had always rested assured that they lived in the tower, not knowing that it had been destroyed.

In an earlier chapter in his autobiography, a foreshadowing of the prison revelation, Malcolm X writes that

> Shorty would take me to groovy, frantic scenes in different chicks' and cats' pads, where with the lights and juke down mellow, everybody blew gage and juiced back and jumped. I met chicks who were fine as May wine, and cats who were hip to all happenings.
>
> That paragraph is deliberate, of course; it's just to display a bit more of the slang that was used by everyone I respected as "hip" in those days. And in no time at all, I was talking slang like a lifelong hipster. (56)

At one level, these two paragraphs serve simply as character development: they add nuance to the man at the center of the autobiography. Yet they also, and more importantly, again reveal Malcolm X's awareness of Babel. At the beginning of chapter 5, the autobiography allows for a theoretical moment of reflection on the nature of language, on the languages in which Malcolm X chose to live. The hipster slang, he reminds his readers here, was, in fact, new to him. It was not his originary dialect, not his home language. Thus, one sees in the autobiography at least three dialects in the Babel of contemporary America, three systems Malcolm X negotiated in his life: the dialect he spoke prior to hipster slang, hipster slang, and SAE. It also reveals that Malcolm X chose SAE as a way to rise above the babble, to speak beyond the confines of the particular communities.

This is not to say that he became European American. Rather, SAE became a way to rise above the limitations of Babel, the limitations of parochially defined language communities, and speak as an African American to the dominant society. SAE, then, served a dual function. It was a way to transcend the Babel of languages and dialects and move into SAE communities. It also provided Malcolm X with a way to challenge these SAE communities, thus reminding all concerned that the unity provided by SAE was a chimera: divisions still existed, and Malcolm X wanted to exacerbate them.

Malcolm X was also aware that language entails not only grammatical structure; it entails, as well, worldviews. Speaking to a group of young civil rights workers in 1965 Mississippi, Malcolm X emphasized that "good relations" depended on communication, and that communication depended on "a language, a common language." He told the young workers that "you can never talk French to somebody who speaks only German and think you're communicating. . . . You have to be able to speak a man's language in order to make him get the point" (*Malcolm X Talks* 61).

He draws this analogy in order to introduce his main idea. Malcolm X does not refer to the conflict between French and German as if it has literal meaning for the members of his audience. Rather, he uses this dilemma in order to highlight the dilemma that these young workers faced: they had to negotiate differences in worldviews as they are embodied in language. Shifting to the workers' other, the Ku Klux Klan, Malcolm X argued:

> You've lived in Mississippi long enough to know what the language of the Ku Klux Klan is. They only know one language. If you come up with another language, you don't communicate. You've got to be able to speak the same language they speak. . . . When you develop or mature to the point where you can speak another man's language on his level, that man gets the point. That's the only time he gets the point. You can't talk peace to a person who doesn't know what peace

means. You can't talk love to a person who doesn't know what love means. (61–62)

Obviously, when Malcolm X uses the word "language" in this passage, he means something more than English, something more than the standard form of English he devoted himself to in prison. By "language" he means the worldview held by the people who use, ostensibly, the same form of English. This level of language is marked by discordance: there is a Babel of worldviews pervading, and pervaded by, English.

Malcolm X realized in prison that those who want to rise above the babble must move out of their own worldviews into others in order to communicate. In this case, he says, it is a matter of maturity, or development. The mature person is one who is able to "speak another man's language on his level." The members of the KKK, needless to say, are not mature. They live in the parochial realm of their own language, unable to understand the worldview the post-Mecca Malcolm X had begun to explore: peace, love, even nonviolence. Knowing this, Malcolm X tells his audience that they must become linguistically mature and realize two things.

First, they must realize that the KKK simply doesn't understand their worldview, and, thus, if the workers would communicate with the KKK, they must mature, develop into sophisticated users of language who can speak to all peoples. Second, and this certainly marks the difference between even the post-Mecca Malcolm X and Martin Luther King Jr., the workers should not try to speak of love and nonviolence to the KKK. The workers must speak the language of the KKK, which is a language of power and of strength. Assuming this worldview, the workers would speak of the right of African Americans to "band together and equip ourselves and qualify ourselves to protect ourselves" (62).

Malcolm X, linguistically mature, recognizes the American Babel and is willing to search for a common language, be it at the level of dialect or worldview. Nonetheless, he does not forfeit his standing as an African American who has suffered, whose ancestors have suffered, at the hands of those who speak SAE, at the hands of those who speak the worldview of the Klan. Malcolm X, simply because he can speak an "American" language, does not believe that he is American.

This, certainly, is a major difference between Malcolm X and King and Du Bois. The latter two always presume their status as Americans; they presume that they are already citizens of the American republic. Malcolm X, though he may use the language of the republic, views himself as an outsider. In fact, Malcolm X holds that the civil rights movement itself proves that he is not an American, that birth alone did not assure him rights. After all, he says, if he was an American, he wouldn't need special legislation, amendments to the Constitution, and the like in order to make him one (*Malcolm X Speaks* 26). So, even though Malcolm X assumes more "universal" languages, he keeps his specific identity as a member of an oppressed group, as a descendant of slaves, as a stranger to the American republic (*Last Speeches* 27).

This, without doubt, accounts for a move Malcolm X made toward the end of his life, after his conversion experience at Mecca. Having recognized the discordance of languages in America, he moved into yet another level of universal language; he added another floor to his tower. Tired of the slow progress of the civil rights movement in America, fearful that African Americans would never achieve justice because European Americans would always control the language of change (*Malcolm X Speaks* 34–35), Malcolm X began to push the case for African Americans at the world level. In short, he wanted the movement not to use the term "civil rights," a term entrapped in an unjust republic. He pressed, instead, for "human rights" as the guiding term. With SAE he moved an "American" worldview into a global one. With this, he claimed, he could "take the case of the black man in this country before the nations in the U.N." where, he claimed, people of color from around the globe are waiting to aid African Americans (*Malcolm X Speaks* 34–35).

While this issue will be treated more in depth in chapters 3 and 4, it is important to emphasize here the movement Malcolm X made through the Babel of the American experience. Once he was a parochial member of a slang-speaking discourse community, unaware, finally, that other communities existed. By the end of his life Malcolm X had, as he would put it, matured. He had moved through

levels of universalization, from SAE to the languages of his antagonists and finally to a level of language beyond the American republic
itself. Malcolm X had come to claim that the republic is linguistically
incapable of adjudicating the dispute between African Americans and
European Americans: its language is too limited. Only when the African American rights movement moved beyond "civil" into "human" could there be hope for just change.

Like Malcolm X, Du Bois recognized the Babel of the American
experience as it was involved in the color line. Throughout the pages
of the *Crisis*, Du Bois revealed the discordancy of American languages
and sought a universal language that would help African Americans
achieve justice. Unlike Malcolm X, Du Bois, a small-town New En-
glander by birth, holder of two college degrees and two Ph.D.'s, never
personally lived the profound disjuncture of American English dialects. Nonetheless, Du Bois was keenly aware of linguistic discordancy, especially as it related to the line. Following is part of his discussion of the word "Negro" from the March 1913 *Crisis* editorial
entitled "An Open Letter to Woodrow Wilson":

> They [Wilson's southern supporters] "know the Negro," as they will
> continually tell you. And this is true. They do know "the Negro," but
> the question for you to settle is whether or not the Negro whom they
> know is the real Negro or the Negro of their vivid imaginations and
> violent prejudices. (*Selections* 1: 51–52)

Du Bois wrote this editorial on the occasion of Wilson's inaugura-
tion as president of the United States. Though Wilson was "a Southerner in birth and tradition," a member of the party that had fought
"to keep black men as real estate in the eyes of the law," and was
once the president of whites-only Princeton, Du Bois felt that Wilson
could help to solve "this burning human wrong" of the color line.
Wilson should do so, Du Bois tells him, for two reasons. The first,
pragmatically political, was that African Americans were beginning
to vote in large numbers and had, in fact, voted for Wilson. Thus,
Wilson could begin to develop strong relationships with a potentially
powerful constituency. The second reason was philosophical. Wilson
must act to lift the veil of the color line because such an action would
fulfill the sacrifices made by both European Americans and African

Americans throughout the history of the republic. Such an action would, according to Du Bois, fulfill the "highest ideals of American Democracy" (*Selections* 1: 51–52).

This second reason is especially important in the context of this book because it reveals Du Bois's awareness of the violence at the heart of the American experiment and also his belief, which Malcolm X denied, that the continued emancipation of African Americans was demanded by the fact that they are Americans. Like King, Du Bois appeals to the American rhetorical heritage. One can almost hear the refrain "land where our fathers died" in this editorial. One can almost see the opening words of the Declaration of Independence, the text of the Emancipation Proclamation (earlier in the editorial, Du Bois does allude to Lincoln, claiming that Wilson could be his heir). At the same time, however, Du Bois emphasizes the violence at the core of the American republic. As will be discussed more fully below, Du Bois infuses his texts with the violence that constitutes the color line.

Wilson, if he is going to heed these political and philosophical reasons provided by Du Bois, needs to start by delving into the discordant language of the American republic. There, according to Du Bois, he will discover a fundamental problem: the definition of "the Negro" is open to question.[3] Wilson's southern friends, Du Bois tells him, have one definition of "the Negro," a definition formed by "vivid imaginations" and "violent prejudices." In order to heighten the issue of definition, at one point in the editorial Du Bois claims that these southern European Americans define "the Negro" as "beasts of fiction." Thus, the struggle over "the Negro" is, profoundly, a struggle over language itself. American racists have created a web of untruths, metamorphosing "the Negro" into something removed from reality.

Du Bois and others define "the Negro" much differently. Wilson, Du Bois thinks, is apt to believe his southern friends if only for the reason that Wilson himself has had "peculiar lack of personal acquaintance with individual black men." The solution to this discordancy of voices, to this Babel that infuses "the Negro," is for Wilson to come to know the Negro "personally" (*Selections* 1: 51–52). That is to say, Du Bois wants Wilson to explore the meaning of this contested term not in the fictions of his southern friends, not even in the language of Du

Bois's editorials, but in the flesh of African Americans as they live and work and die in the republic.

This passage from the letter to Wilson reveals Du Bois's awareness of the double nature of Babel. He recognizes the discordancy of language, that there are competing discourses. At the same time, he offers a way out of the morass of discordancy.[4] Clearly, he is not content to let "the Negro" serve as a site of the discordancy of Babel. He has a definition of the term, to which he only hints in this editorial, that counters the southerner's definition. He wants Wilson to share his own definition, which would, because Wilson is the president of the United States, make this definition "universal." This is not to say that the discordancy of voices would disappear immediately. However, if the president of the United States "speaks a certain language" and pushes for its realization in social policy, it will, perhaps, become a universal code for the republic. At the very least, its chances for universality are greater than if it were being promoted only by Du Bois.

Du Bois, like Malcolm X, was not content to depend upon the universalization of certain languages within the American experience. In addition to seeking the ascendancy, in America, of definitions of American terms like "the Negro," Du Bois sought an international, universal language that could help African Americans in their struggle with the color line.

Arising from both his interpretation of World War I and his desire for a pan-African movement (which will be discussed more fully in chapter 4), Du Bois claimed that "any effective *rapprochement pan-africain* must depend . . . on the ability of the groups of the Negro race to make themselves mutually understood throughout the world" (*Selections* 1: 181). Du Bois had come to believe that the American color line could be effectively addressed only by an internationalist movement. However, he also recognized that the Babel of language was not simply an American affair, separating European Americans and African Americans over terms like "the Negro." All peoples of African descent, be they in America or France or South America or Africa itself, were divided by Babel. While they shared an ancestry and the experience of slavery, these peoples could not speak to one another.

In order to overcome this linguistic division, Du Bois came to propose, following World War I, that "every Negro should speak French. Large numbers should speak Spanish and Portuguese" (1: 181). Du Bois chose these languages—French, Spanish, and Portuguese—for two reasons, it seems. Albeit with naive romanticism, he claimed that "the only white civilization in the world to which color-hatred is not only unknown, but absolutely unintelligible is the so-called Latin, of which France and Spain are the leading nations" (1: 181).[5] Du Bois, then, is still hoping to salvage from "white civilization" a way to a better future, a future without the color line. As numerous students of Du Bois have observed, he was, through and through, a man of European heritage.

Unlike Malcolm X, who claimed that he spoke as a black man and not as an American, that he was, in fact, not American (let alone European), Du Bois looks to "white civilization" for, literally in this case, a *lingua franca* that can overcome the Babel in which people of African descent find themselves. Latin languages, Du Bois claims, provide this tower because the cultures in which they are embedded are not tainted by the color line. In contrast, English and its Anglo-Saxon culture is incapable, finally, of providing a means to overcome linguistic discordance.[6]

Like Malcolm X, Du Bois steps outside of the American rhetorical heritage in order to call into question the American rhetorical heritage itself. Du Bois doesn't entirely reject the American tradition, as his letter to Wilson shows. However, the tradition is finally linguistically inadequate to the challenge of the color line.

Du Bois also chooses French, Spanish, and Portuguese—in particular the first two—because they are already languages of most "educated people of Negro descent" (*Selections* 1: 181).[7] Numerically as well as ideologically, then, English is inadequate to the task of social justice for African Americans. Du Bois seeks strength in numbers and finds that strength outside of his native tongue. A master of the English language itself, Du Bois suggests that America is incomplete without foreign language, without the other.

Like Malcolm X and Du Bois, King also well understood the Babel of America. His work is rife with the recognition that America comprises discordant voices, all linked to the problem of the color line. He too seeks a towering language that can overcome the discordancy and finds it not in internationalization, as Malcolm X and Du Bois finally do, but in the voices of the American political and so-called Judeo-Christian tradition. This is hardly an original observation. Even a casual reading of King reveals his use of these two traditions. Lischer claims, quite correctly, that "King responded to the events in Montgomery by interpreting their meaning in relation to American history, the Constitution, and the Bible" (198).

As is the case for Du Bois in his editorials, King's recognition of the discordancy of languages shows up most evidently in his concern about definitions.[8] This quotation, taken from King's final presidential address to the Southern Christian Leadership Conference, speaks to this issue:

> Even semantics have conspired to make that which is black seem ugly and degrading. In Roget's *Thesaurus*, there are 120 synonyms for blackness and at least sixty of them are offensive, as for example, blot, soot, grim, devil and foul. And there are some 134 synonyms for whiteness and all are favorable, expressed in such words as purity, cleanliness, chastity and innocence. A white lie is better than a black lie. The most degenerate member of a family is a "black sheep." Ossie Davis has suggested that maybe the English language should be reconstructed so that teachers will not be forced to teach the Negro child sixty ways to despise himself, and thereby perpetuate his false sense of inferiority, and the white child 134 ways to adore himself, and thereby perpetuate his false sense of superiority. (245–46)

The brilliance of this observation, coming as it did toward the end of King's life, is its sophisticated reflection on the nature of the American Babel. First, as King understands it, Babel is real and is found even at the level of single words. Like Du Bois, King understands that individual words themselves are sites of contention. Clearly, King, among others, disagrees vehemently with the web of associations that *Roget's Thesaurus* has discovered in this term. King recognized that individual words point to other words. All words are involved in a chain of meaning, and these meanings are produced by human beings who often disagree with one another about the meaning of a word.

Furthermore, as King makes clear in this passage, words are linked to other words in the form of sentences. These sentences, too, are sites of contention, revelations of the discord of language and the color line at the heart of the American experience. "Why," King implicatingly asks, "does 'black sheep' connote bad or even evil? What effects do these connotations have on Negroes?" His answer comes by way of a reference to the actor Ossie Davis: these connotations teach African Americans to despise themselves. King, obviously, challenges these connotations and, necessarily, the communities of discourse in which these connotations have positive meaning.

Moreover, King understands that language, as a discordant site of contention, is woven systematically into the fabric of American life. *Roget's Thesaurus,* for instance, is not a haphazard choice. It is a standard reference tool in American culture. King suggests that while words like "blackness" are sites of discordancy, of disagreement, the reference system actually supports the racist interpretations of these words. Encoded in a leading reference work, after all, are connotations that support the color line. King, near the end of his life, working amidst a fractured civil rights movement in an America deeply involved in Vietnam, knows that the standard language supports the color line. Thus, he raises the idea, albeit fleetingly and suggestively, that the English language itself needs to be restructured.

Ironically, King himself was trapped by this system, as is evident in his 1961 interpretation of the mission of Jesus. King argues that Jesus precipitated a struggle "between the forces of light and the forces of darkness" (51). The forces of light, following the traditional pattern, are, of course, associated with the kingdom of God. The forces of darkness, then, imply the opposite. Even King, aware as he was of the systemic racism embodied in language, was trapped by it. His own metaphors present light as good, dark as bad. Through attention to the discordant voices found at the level of individual words and phrases, King calls into question our literate culture itself. As King came to understand it late in his life, literate culture, represented by a book like *Roget's Thesaurus,* excludes African Americans.

Du Bois, at least at one point in his life, opts out of English completely, arguing for the ascendancy of languages that are not systematically racist. It is, of course, impossible to say what King might have moved toward had he lived. Throughout his work, however, one finds that King did discover a new language tower in the midst of the Babel of tongues. In "The Case Against 'Tokenism,' " a 1962 *New York Times Magazine* piece, King holds that

> [i]f the inexpressible cruelties of slavery could not extinguish our existence, the opposition we now face will surely fail. We feel that we are the conscience of America—we are its troubled soul. We will continue to insist that right be done because both God's will and the heritage of our nation speak through our echoing demands. (111)

The towering language is that of African Americans themselves. King, not incidentally, echoes here liberation theology, a movement that privileges the voices of the oppressed. While African Americans speak in an oppositional atmosphere, challenged by others who echo the history of slavery, King suggests that the African American voice —hence the first person plural "we"—has been ordained both by God and by American history to overcome the Babel of the color line and move America toward social justice.

The ordination of the African American voice, as King understands it, cannot be overemphasized. This voice gains its legitimacy from the fact that forces greater than it—God and the ideals of justice embedded in the republic—validate its desires. This observation is not new. What perhaps has not been emphasized enough is the linguistic slant King provides. Elsewhere he speaks of

> a voice crying out in terms that echo across the generations, saying: Love your enemies, bless them that curse you, pray for them that despitefully use you, that you may be the children of your Father which is in Heaven. (139–40)

This voice, without doubt, allusively belongs to Jesus Christ. It is a voice that validates, so King holds, his own voice and the voices of all African Americans who would work with him. Significantly, he uses a quotation that emphasizes not only the legitimating voice of Jesus but also a quotation that directs African Americans to linguistic action: bless, pray.

So too King claims that the voices of such figures as Amos, Lincoln, Jefferson, and Christ call members of the movement to action.

King creates a bulwark of voices that support his tower amidst the Babel of contentious languages surrounding the color line. King's tower is supported by the voices of the Judeo-Christian tradition and America calling him, and the republic, to overcome the color line.

Division of Property

As Burke suggests in his rhetorical reinterpretation of the Fall, Babel is accompanied by property division: just as humans suffer communicative discordance, so too they suffer division in the economic structures of their lives. This is not to say that Babel has caused property division, or that property division has caused Babel. As Burke understands the Fall rhetorically, each causes and is caused by the other.

Burke is most often concerned about property division in general, but he is well aware that it has specific manifestations, that it is linked to specific locales, specific problems, including that of the color line in America. This is made evident in *A Rhetoric of Motives*, coming to the surface during a discussion of "ultimate terms" in Marxist dialectic. From a Marxist perspective, Burke reminds his readers that the "Negro in America" was "an extremely underprivileged class" (193). This is to say that in terms of "the Fall," the oppression of African Americans is intricately linked to the division of property and the social classes that are linked to this divided property in one way or another.

So too the compositional strategy of Malcolm X reveals an awareness that the color line in the American republic is not caused simply by Babel. It is also caused by property division, a division that separates not only European Americans from African Americans but also African Americans from African Americans. Michael Dyson holds that Malcolm X recognized that classism was at the root of racism (100–101), but it is not clear that this is the case. While Malcolm X understood class to be an integral part of racism, it is not clear that he thought classism caused racism.

In a speech delivered not long before his death, Malcolm X referred to this issue in general, attempting to differentiate himself from the civil rights movement led by King and others. While the post-

Mecca Malcolm X had begun to seek rapprochement with "the movement," he still believed that his own vision differed significantly on many issues, including the end of "the Negro revolt." Malcolm X held that this revolt would merge into a more global revolution of all "black" people (by which he meant, at this point in his life, nonwhites). In so doing, African Americans would come to realize that the revolt would need to become a revolution. Instead of struggling "for an integrated cup of coffee," they would be engaged in a struggle over land. As Malcolm X reminded his audience, the worldwide decolonization movement was centered on property: the indigenous people of color throughout the world sought to regain their lands from the European colonizers (*Malcolm X Speaks* 49–50).

In many of his speeches, Malcolm X brought this property division to bear on the color line in America itself. It wasn't simply peoples in the so-called third world who had been economically oppressed by Europeans; African Americans also suffered under the oppressive property practices of European Americans. For instance, in a speech to a group at Oxford, he claimed that "I live in a society whose . . . economy is based upon the castration of the Black man" (*Malcolm X Talks* 21–22).[9] While this speech does not explain this comment, the comment clearly alludes to slavery and its horrible legacy in the lives of African Americans. Malcolm X presumes that the point doesn't need detailed reflection, only comments like "the government has shown its inability, or its unwillingness, to do whatever is necessary to protect life and property where the Black American is concerned" (22).

In another speech delivered in England, this time at the London School of Economics, Malcolm X spoke more directly, and at greater length, about the interconnectedness of the color line and property division:

> In America the Black community in which we live is not owned by us. The landlord is white. The merchant is white. In fact, the entire economy of the Black community in the States is controlled by someone who doesn't even live there. The property that we live in is owned by someone else. The store that we trade in is operated by someone else. And these are the people who suck the economic blood of our community. (*Malcolm X Talks* 29)

Not incidentally, this sentiment, expressed by Malcolm X in 1965, was also explored by Spike Lee in his film *Do the Right Thing*. An Italian American father and his two sons own and operate a pizzeria in an African American community in New York City but live elsewhere. Decorating the walls of the restaurant are pictures of Italian American notables. A local activist leads a struggle to convince the restaurant to become more responsive to the community in which it makes its money. One request the activist makes is that the restaurant include pictures of African American notables on the walls. Much of the film is an exploration of the property tensions of the color line.

In addition to the tensions between Italian Americans and African Americans, Lee explores as well a dimension of the color line new to our own time: the property struggles between African Americans and Korean Americans who are now running stores in African American neighborhoods in cities like New York. The film includes a grocery store managed by recent Korean immigrants who have, at best, an uneasy relationship with the neighborhood. Malcolm X would, perhaps, be shocked by the tensions between Korean and African Americans. As will be discussed more fully in chapter 3, by the end of his life Malcolm X had come to envision a global union of people of color. "Black" came to include all non-whites. Significantly, Lee's film ends with a riot scene, and the Italian restaurant (but not the Korean grocery) is destroyed by enraged African Americans. The Italians were understood by the African Americans to be those leeches who "suck the economic blood" from the community.

The verb metaphor—"suck the economic blood"—Malcolm X allusively uses to describe those who control African American property both dehumanizes and demonizes the European Americans. One of this metaphor's allusions is to the mosquito, the leech, or other creatures that flourish parasitically by drinking human blood. However, this metaphor contains another allusion, one with much more sinister meaning: the vampire. One cannot read this speech fully unless one is able to move within the web of Malcolm X's allusive literacy. The verb metaphor takes an astute reader not only into the world of parasitic creatures but also into the myths and legends of the vampire, leading to Bela Lugosi, Anne Rice, and Bram Stoker. In so doing, this metaphor also challenges the oppressive American system. It takes the "white man" and all of its usual associated meanings—revealed so well by King in his discussion of "blackness" in *Roget's Thesaurus*—and inverts it. "White" is, in Malcolm X's thesaurus, involved in a web that would damage the psyches of white schoolchildren were they to learn it. They would come to think of themselves as the parasitic vampires who suck the economic lifeblood from suffering African Americans.

While he saw that the color line included a race-based division of property, separating European Americans and African Americans, Malcolm X also believed that the color line drove a property gulf between African Americans, as well. Malcolm X's "house Negro/field Negro" is his most famous description of this problem (see *Last Speeches* 28–30; *Malcolm X Speaks* 10–12, *End* 87). Essentially, Malcolm X thinks that African Americans have been divided by the European American economic system. The house Negroes identify with the European Americans, desirous of their wealth, power, and culture. In short, the house Negroes want to be white. In contrast, the field Negroes—the masses, Malcolm X claims—hate the masters and want to see the current social system, based on the racial division of property, end.[10]

Like Malcolm X, Du Bois understood that property division was intimately linked to the color line. For Du Bois, the division lies primarily between African Americans and two classes of European Americans: the owners and the working class. In a strong editorial regarding the property relationship between the European American owners and African American workers, Du Bois cast the relationship in aggressive language. Writing about coal mine strikes in Kentucky and Pennsylvania, Du Bois places the European American and African American workers together. Both struggle against a common foe: the owner. As will be discussed below, this unity between workers does not last. However, for this moment, Du Bois claims that these united workers "have stood up staunchly for a living wage, for freedom of speech, for the abolition of feudalism" (*Selections* 2: 659).

Here, Du Bois claims that America, despite its capitalist facade, is, in fact, marked by feudalism. The mine owners become nobility, the miners themselves indentured peasants bound to the owner and land. "Feudalism" is not simply an artifact of history for Du Bois; it is not vocabulary needed only for school study. Rather, it is part of the contemporary American order, bringing to the republic the taint of an unjust system.

Elsewhere, Du Bois is less metaphorical, more scientific, in his discussions of the link between property and the color line. A 1911 editorial lauds the property gains made by African Americans but also decries a system that tries to stymie African American gain. Du Bois uses statistics garnered from various sources to prove that African Americans, once thought of as "indolent tropical being[s]," "inborn" with "laziness," had made enormous gains. In Georgia, for instance, they had secured "$30,000,000 worth of property." However, Du Bois argues, these gains are under constant threat. He claims, for instance, that "the lower courts" are organized in such a way as to make it "often impossible" for African Americans "to defend their property rights" (*Selections* 1: 3–8).

As problematic as the property relationships between owners and workers are, Du Bois is also troubled by the relationship between European American workers and African American workers. It too is marked by the property division at the color line. Both share much, Du Bois argues in one editorial, mainly "complaints against capitalists" (*Selections* 2: 697). However, African American labor suffers at the hands of European American labor. The latter group, Du Bois claims, "deprives the Negro of his right to vote, denies him education, denies him affiliation with trade unions, expels him from decent houses and neighborhoods, and heaps upon him the public insults of open color discrimination" (2: 697). European American workers do this, finally, because they want to "climb to wealth on the backs of black labor," a group comprising most African Americans, a group that has suffered slavery, disenfranchisement, and the "Color Bar" (2: 698).

Like Du Bois, King recognized, at least as early as May 1960, that "the Negro has remained the poor, the underprivileged, and the lowest class" (96). The economic status of this class arises, as King narrates in a typical King sweep of history, from the beginning of the colonization of America. King reminds readers in a 1957 essay published in the *Christian Century* that Africans arrived on the shores of America one year before the Pilgrim fathers, but they arrived in chains (5–6). African slaves became property in order to work the property of their masters, and the history of African Americans is always marked by this fact. The Dred Scott decision of 1857 made this situation legal, and, while the Civil War and subsequent laws undid this property relationship, African Americans continued to suffer. The 1896 Plessy decision, King reminds his readers, powerfully reinstituted slavery. It plunged "the Negro into the abyss of exploitation where he experienced the bleakness of nagging injustice" (6).

King understood this abyss of injustice to be multidimensional, including the problematics of housing, voting rights, segregation in business practice, segregation on intercity and interstate forms of transportation, and the like. Yet, "the movement" was not simply about the end of segregation, about the ability of European Americans and Africans, to borrow from Rodney King's recent nationwide plea, "to just get along." King understood that "the movement," in a fundamental sense, was about economics, was about the relationship of the division of property to the color line. Why else, for instance, should he speak about African Americans as being the lowest class? Why else should he recount African American history as a history of property relationships?

Dyson claims that the late King recognized classism at the root of racism (100–101), but as early as 1961 King was fully linking "the movement" to the question of property relationships, was fully beginning to explore the relationships between property divisions and the color line. This is evidently manifest in a speech delivered to the AFL-CIO. Like Du Bois, King recognized that the color line not only divided workers from owners; it also divided workers (King 205–6).

King argued that "Negroes are almost entirely a working people," and thus the concerns of the labor union movement are the concerns of African Americans. Facing these allies, King maintains, is a resurgent, reactionary force (including "big military and big industry," "a coalition of southern dixiecrats and northern reactionaries") that wants to "regain the despotism" of the nineteenth century while "retaining the wealth and privileges of the twentieth century" (203). For King, fundamental to "the movement" is a struggle against that old Marxist trope, "the owners."

King seeks, finally, a radical reorganization of the American republic; his composition is aimed at an emancipatory ideal. For here, it is enough merely to quote King's vision, a vision at odds with the construction of property relations in King's time, a vision at odds with the construction of property relations as the twenty-first century nears:

> This will be the day when we shall bring into full realization the American dream—a dream yet unfilled. A dream of equality of opportunity, of privilege and property widely distributed; a dream of a land where men will not take necessities from the many to give luxuries to the few; a dream of a land where men will not argue that the color of a man's skin determines the content of his character; a dream of a nation where all our gifts and resources are held not for ourselves alone but as instruments of service for the rest of humanity; the dream of a country where every man will respect the dignity and worth of human personality—that is the dream. (206)

Violence

King recognized, however, that he and the union would have to work for this dream in a country prone to violence, in a country that would probably not join the dreamers with language honed in a school of composition but with physical violence that might even lead to death (206–7). King well understood, as did Malcolm X and Du Bois, that the American republic's color line, marked as it was by the Babel of language and property division, was a line of violence as well. As Burke discusses in his rhetorical treatment of the Fall, physical violence is part of the post-Edenic mess.

Cone has discussed the dynamics of physical violence in the lives and work of Malcolm X and King in great detail. To add to that discussion, it is necessary to focus on how these two, and Du Bois, included physical violence in their compositions and on what strategies they used to name the legacy of slavery in order to work for the emancipation of their people.

Physical violence—in fact the explicit naming of physical violence—is a dominant theme in Malcolm X's work. Malcolm X sees physical violence at the heart of the American republic, part of the color line itself. He knows that European Americans bloody African Americans. He also calls on African Americans to respond in kind, if need be. The latter is part of the American republic's common knowledge about Malcolm X, most graphically depicted on the poster and T-shirt picture of him holding a rifle and standing at a window above the words "By any means necessary."

The former facet, Malcolm X's understanding of the physical violence suffered by African Americans, is actually a richer part of his work, and it is not surprising that it has not accompanied the myth of Malcolm X into the American republic's common knowledge. Consider, for instance, this passage from the speech that he delivered at the founding rally of the Organization of Afro-American Unity:

> It is the duty of every Afro-American person and every Afro-American community throughout this country to protect its people against mass murderers, against bombers, against lynchers, against floggers, against brutalizers and against exploiters. (*By Any Means* 42)

While this passage reveals the Malcolm X who would physically hurt European Americans, it also reminds its readers that he always placed such violence in the context of response: he would act violently only if acted upon violently. Moreover, this passage reveals a typical compositional strategy. While he points to very real sorts of physical violence—such as lynching—he often speaks in the abstract. Here, for instance, he mentions no actual cases. He refers only to what might happen, what African Americans might expect to happen, given the country's history.

Elsewhere, he speaks of violent acts of the past, such as "skulls crushed" by the KKK, but again he makes no specific reference to actual events (*Malcolm X Talks* 24). While the events did, of course, happen, Malcolm X relies on his audience's ability to work allusively, to take these words and make the historical connections on their own. By not pointing to specific instances, Malcolm X leaves open this question: How frequently did this violence occur? His audience is left to let the incidents grow or shrink in frequency as their personal experience and conjecture lead them.

Du Bois also sometimes alludes to violence, leaving it up to the readers of the *Crisis* to make meaningful connections between Du

Bois's rhetoric and the world of bodies being hurt. This tactic appears, for instance, in the May 1911 editorial about property, a portion of which was discussed above. At the end of the piece, Du Bois maintains that one of the great problems that African American property holders face is that of mob violence (*Selections* 1: 7–8). While he locates this in the South, he leaves locations unspecified, names unnamed.

However, Du Bois also specifically names violent events, leaving his readers no doubt about the location and the actors. Du Bois, throughout his editorials, was overwhelmingly concerned about lynching, in particular. In an early editorial titled "The Lynching Industry," Du Bois provides tables to speak to this concern (*Selections* 1: 88–90). One lists the "Colored Men Lynched in 1914" by state and name; another lists the number of lynchings that occurred in each month and that occurred in each state; another, the number of lynchings that occurred each year from 1885 to 1914, totaling 2,732. Clearly, Du Bois did not leave sociology behind when he became editor of the *Crisis*. He uses typical social scientific strategy—numbers, tables, and the like—to depict the physically violent act of lynching.

Following the tables, though, are a series of short narratives, relating to readers a number of specific lynching cases. One speaks of a young African American girl who was raped by two European Americans. Her brother killed one of the rapists, Du Bois reports, and, in retaliation, the rapists' friends "*lynched the girl.*" The italicization of "lynched the girl" introduces absurdity into the narrative. Du Bois is dumbfounded that this was the response. It is almost as if one can hear Du Bois saying, "Can you believe it? They *lynched the girl.*"

Violence is also rife throughout King's work. Like Du Bois, he both alludes to violence in general and focuses on specific cases. Unlike Du Bois, however, King relies on the narrative play of a preacher, not the statistical skills of a sociologist. Speaking of the students who led the lunch-counter sit-ins, King tells his audience at a 1961 commencement address that "these people have been beaten" (214). Unlike Malcolm X, King does not offer specific description. He does not tell his audience, for instance, that the students had their skulls crushed. Like Du Bois, however, King locates the violence in a specific place with specific people. He directs his audience to an event they may have already seen played out through the media or even in person.

So too in a later piece King maintains the specificity of people and place. Describing the travails of movement members, he tells his readers they have suffered "broken bodies and bloody heads." He goes on to speak of one Sheriff Clark of Dallas County who

> forced an inhuman march upon hundreds of Negro children; who ordered the Reverend James Bevel chained to his sickbed; who clubbed a Negro woman registrant, and who callously inflicted repeated brutalities and indignities upon nonviolent Negroes peacefully petitioning for their constitutional right to vote. (184)

The audience of the speech is immediately located in a specific place with specific people. "In case you didn't know this," King seems to suggest, "look to Sheriff Clark and Dallas County. There you will see the effects of the color line. There you will see the ways in which the American republic is marked by the color line, the color line not only of Babel, not only of property division, but the color line of physical violence, the color line of physical pain. Is this not the Fall?"

3 | The Orient

I am, after all, composing about people of another race
and a radically different heritage.

— Wendell Berry, *The Hidden Wound*

Despite the divisions marked by the Fall, many contemporary theorists, echoing Donne—not to mention Simon and Gar-
funkel—argue that it is not possible to live as a fortress island: the
other always impinges upon the self. In fact, the other and the self are
always involved in mutual definition. As Burke would hold, there is
no self without the other, no other without the self; terms necessarily
carry within themselves their opposites. For the age of Du Bois, King,
and Malcolm X, "America" as a member of the "Occident," as perhaps its leading member, implies the "Orient."

The realization of the linguistic importance of the Orient poses
significant questions, however, for Americans seeking to preserve and
strengthen the republic. Does the Orient exist only so the Occident,
in particular the American republic, can construct itself as different
from it, as superior to it? Or, does it exist as a dialectical partner,
something that calls into question the Occident and thus its epitome,
the American republic itself?

The former question, and its answer, is articulated brilliantly by
Edward Said. He demarcates three typical Western responses to the
Orient (2–4). The first marks academicians who study things Orien-
tal, from the Middle East to the Far East. The second highlights writ-
ers whose work is informed by a distinction between East and West.
The third area is even more pernicious than the first two and in fact
often pervades them: the Orient is constructed in such a way that the
Occident can dominate it. In general, Said argues that the entire
Western enterprise of "Orientalism" has been a failure, an act of intellectual and human reductionism. Said seeks a way to approach the
Orient that avoids reductionism, that is able to avoid the alienation
common to most approaches to the Orient (328).

Although Said concentrates his study on the efforts of the British and French in relation to the Middle East, or the Near East, his argument soundly speaks to the condition of the American republic. Too often, the term Orient is not taken as a dialectical partner, an allusive word that provides critical insight into the preservation and fruitful growth of the republic. Too often, its composition alludes to webs of meaning that are alien to America, webs that work not for emancipation but for oppression. America, as a culture, often composes the Orient oppressively. Three typical webs of meaning to which the word alludes in America are a yellow, alien other, a wise person, and a backward place.

As an allusive term, the Orient represents a heterogeneous mixture of cultures while it simultaneously represents a general category of human being. Just as there is an Occident—a German and an American look more alike than a German and a Korean; American culture shares more with English than it does with Japanese—there is an Orient. However, in any sort of ontologically meaningful way, there is no Orient. Nonetheless, American discourse tends ontologically to construct an Orient in both less offensive and more offensive ways.

Awareness of heterogeneity, or the lack of awareness of heterogeneity, is one reason many young African American men feel compelled to speak fake Chinese (or at least pseudo-Chinese language), for instance, to a Korean American woman. They see her as an "Oriental," which, for them, means Chinese. They are, it seems, unaware that there is no "Oriental" person. There are Koreans, Japanese, Chinese, Burmese, and the list could go on and on.

So too a European American T'ai Chi teacher, when he learned that a Korean American acquaintance of his was not interested in learning this Chinese psychosomatic art, despaired with this comment: "It's her culture. Doesn't she want to keep it alive?" The obvious point is that T'ai Chi is Chinese in origin, not Korean.

Another example is this: in military dialect, at least among the U.S. Marines, "gook" has come to serve as a general term for all Orientals. Gook arises from the Korean term "Han Gook," which means, roughly, "Korean." An American commonplace, used in reference to people who originate in Oriental countries, "gook" captures the spirit of these allusive webs of meaning: "They all look the same. I can't tell them apart."

Consider, as well, this final, and notorious, example. America incarcerated Japanese Americans during World War II because America did not differentiate Japanese Americans—some of whom had lived in the United States for generations—from the Japanese whom Americans were battling in the Pacific theater. Japanese Americans were incarcerated because America composed "Japanese" as a word with one meaning. America failed to see that individual words are, in fact, phonic and graphic traces of heterogeneity.

Members of the American republic also tend to think of the Orient as the originating source of the wise person. Rooted, no doubt, in Western perceptions of Eastern meditative practices, American culture has composed such figures as Mr. Miyagi, the beneficent karate teacher of the popular *Karate Kid* movie series. Miyagi *Sensei*, in the installment titled *The Next Karate Kid*, comes to the aid of a difficult young woman, the granddaughter of Miyagi *Sensei*'s commanding officer in World War II. She is suffering from the death of her parents and, thus, is quickly becoming a juvenile delinquent: she hates school, stays out late, and treats her loving grandmother with terrible hostility. Miyagi *Sensei*, through enigmatic sayings delivered in broken English, karate practice, and immersion in the silence of a Zen Buddhist monastery, rescues his dear friend's granddaughter, helping to transform her into a caring, loving, but tough, teenager. Before her, he did the same for "Daniel *san*," the hero of the first three movies in the series.

At another level, not incidentally, *The Next Karate Kid* is itself an example of emancipatory composition. The film opens at a dedication ceremony for a memorial created to recall the famous Japanese American unit that fought in the European theater during the war. Thus, Miyagi *Sensei* enters into the girl's problems with his otherness foregrounded. Miyagi fought in a segregated unit for the United States, the country that imprisoned other Japanese Americans. The quintessential American girl, the bright and beautiful yet troubled granddaughter of a war hero, is saved by the only person who can help her: the quiet, enigmatic, wise Japanese American *sensei* who leads her down the path of karate and Zen Buddhism.

So too Isabel Allende composes the quiet, mysterious, wise Oriental. In her novel *The Infinite Plan*, one finds two very wise women: Thui Nguyen, a Vietnamese, and Ming O'Brien, a Taiwanese immigrant to the United States. Thui is the Vietnamese fiancée of Juan José Morales, Vietnam combat infantryman and dear friend of Gregory Reeves, protagonist. After Morales is killed, Reeves goes to visit Thui to give her the news. He "await[s] her arrival with terrible anxiety; he [can]not think how to soften the blow of what he had to tell her." When they meet, Reeves only wants to escape; the two sit in silence. Before Reeves can speak, she "look[s] up at him, her face expressionless." Calmly, even serenely, she tells Reeves that she knows Morales has died. Reeves stammers; his heart fills with tears. He "pound[s] the table with his fist." By the end of the scene, the betrothed, pregnant with Morales's child, offers psychic comfort to Reeves and refuses any money. She is the picture of calm, quiet wisdom (207–8).

This image of Thui is only strengthened later in the novel. Dying, she turns her son, Dai Morales, over to Carmen Morales, Juan José's sister. She does so "lying back on her pillow, peaceful and smiling," while Carmen, "hot tears coursing down her cheeks," declares that Thui has given her "what I have wanted all my life" and promises to be a good mother. Thui "softly" says "we do what we can." Dai, not incidentally and not surprisingly, given this understanding of "Oriental," turns out to be a "prodigy in mathematics" (270).

Ming O'Brien, for her part, serves as Reeves's psychotherapist, "serene and wise among her delicate paintings and fresh flowers" (346). Having "a firm, intelligent gaze that bored" into Reeves's soul (345), she helps him to recreate himself, to become a whole person purified of a lifetime of emotional poison. Even at the end of the novel when Reeves, psychically cured but facing financial ruin, laments his situation, O'Brien succinctly and wisely tells him that "you're losing material things; you'll come out with everything else intact." Reeves tells the reader that "she was right, as always" (380).

Alongside the visions of the homogeneous entity and the wise person is that of the backward place. *City of Hope*, a popular Hollywood movie starring Patrick Swayze as a troubled American doctor who travels to India, certainly composes the Orient as such. The doctor travels to the squalid slums of India in order to "find himself" after a patient of his died on the operating table. Working among lepers and the poor, he heals the sick and sets free the oppressed. Not only does he work in a medical clinic, he also teaches the poor Indians a lesson in American human rights and democracy. With his help, the oppressed slum-dwellers overthrow an evil slum lord.

In a slightly more nuanced and intellectual mode, E. D. Hirsch in his *Cultural Literacy* also composes the Orient as backward. China, for instance, stands as the negative other. He claims that "to this very day, China is a polyglot nation of mutually unintelligible dialects," and, until recently, "in the absence of a standard tongue China was not able to function successfully as a modern industrial and economic unit" (76). In terms of chapter 2, China is still in the state of Babel, which has prevented it from becoming an industrialized nation-state.

Even Japan, to which Hirsch points with some admiration for its high literacy level and economic power (1–2), is found regressive. Although Japan was able to standardize its nonalphabetic script, its system is not as efficient or as easy as Europe's, and thus, by implication, America's (76–77). Japan, China's historical other, is superior to China but inferior to its modern other, Europe.

As Said suggests, the West has often dominated the "Orient" through composition. That is to say, the Orient becomes a matter of language, composed in texts as a way to make "the Orient speak," to render "its mysteries plain for and to the West" (20–21). A poem, for instance, composes the Orient for a reader, and that Orient, as it is presented in the text, may become the Orient the reader knows. Assumed by writer and reader to be true, this composing is a chimera. Drawing on Nietzsche, Said holds that the Orient is always presented in language and that the truth of language is but "'illusions about which one has forgotten that this is what they are'" (203). Or, as he writes, "the written statement is a presence to the reader by virtue of its having excluded, displaced, made supererogatory any such *real thing* as 'the Orient'" (21).

For Said, this act of composing the Orient has, almost always, led to domination. Rather than truly attempting to connect with the human experience that the word marks, writers composing the Orient have set it up as a place of "irreducible opposition," thus making it totally alien to the human experience of the West (328).

Take Allende's Thui Nguyen, for example. At one level, she is an appealing character: serene, capable of extraordinary calm and wisdom in the midst of chaos. While the world about her is destroyed, while her own life is seeping away, she acts like nobody else can act: she is above the fray of human emotion, frailness, fallibility. But this strength is also her weakness as a character. Unlike the central figures of the book, Thui Nguyen is not human: she is the void of Buddhism, that realm beyond suffering and death. While she is a wonderful alien, she is alien nonetheless. She is, finally, irreducibly opposed to the Occident as she encounters it in Reeves and Carmen Morales.

Some might consider the term Oriental itself problematic, a compositional strategy that is reductive and therefore oppressive. Consider, for instance, Dai Morales, the Vietnamese–Mexican American son of Thai Nguyen in Allende's novel. He tells his second mother, Carmen Morales, that "I'm the only moron who calls Orientals Asiatics. . . . I'm the only politically correct person in the whole blessed school" (363). Dai, interracial avatar and mathematical genius, is also portrayed as the bearer of a new language. In his vocabulary, "Oriental" has given way to "Asiatic." This latter term is apparently more in vogue, less demeaning to the Occident's other.

Despite the attempt by Allende and others to refashion American diction, Oriental marks this other of the Occident for two reasons. As Said argues, the phenomenon of Orientalism covers (and as the dictionary definition of the term suggests) lands as diverse as Egypt and Japan. The Orient is not simply what is called the Far East. Moreover, "Oriental" allows one to keep in mind the broad dialectic of Occident/Orient. Asia splinters this dialectic, moves one away from East/West into more local oppositions, such as Asia/America, Asia/Europe, Asia/Africa. "Oriental" allows one to keep in mind a fundamental dialectic at the root of Western composition.

This dialectic is, certainly, at play in the compositions of Du Bois, King, and Malcolm X. Typical Americans, they often compose Orientals as a homogeneous racial entity, as a block of people of color. Yet, they do so in order to work for emancipation. To consider the use of "Oriental" in the works of Du Bois, King, and Malcolm X is to enter into revolutionary play. One is asked to move analogically, in solidarity, to this other in order to find a place from which to call into question the oppressive practices of the American republic. Du Bois, King, and Malcolm X transform the Orient from the alien, homogeneous other of standard American compositions into a place and people who serve as a critique of the color line in America, and thus America itself.

Yellow, Alien Other

Du Bois, at one level, focuses on Asia. It is a site of contest between the powers of Europe and America and of a people of color who need to be freed, brothers and sisters who can strengthen the struggle of African Americans. This quotation from an editorial in the March 1926 *Crisis* speaks to this:

> Make way for the freedom of Asia and Africa. There can be no real disarmament in Europe and America if white nations must hold yellow and black folk in chains and then ever suffer the temptation to throttle each other in order to monopolize their illgotten gains. There can be no freedom and uplift in Philadelphia and America while a conscienceless freebooter like Smed–ley Butler is able to bludgeon helpless West Indians. (*Selections* 2: 435)

Typical of Du Bois's editorials, this fragment presumes that the reader knows the extremely complex situations to which Du Bois alludes, or that the reader is willing to dive into this world, using Du Bois's discourse as a diving board. The Orient—here Asia—parallels Africa, just as yellow parallels black. Thus, Du Bois speaks of yellow people in general, an all-encompassing category of a people of color suffering under European American domination.

The Orient (like Africa) is not simply a site of European American domination, however. As it suffers under this domination, it is also part of a larger global problem. Strangely, as the dominated other, it also causes arms wars. It is coveted by all nations, and, thus, all nations are unwilling to let go of armaments. They jostle continuously with each other for the right to dominate yellow people.

This editorial continues Du Bois's elucidation of a theme he promoted before World War I. At least as early as 1913, he claimed that "the modern lust of land and slaves in . . . Asia . . . is the greatest and almost the only cause of war between the so-called civilized peoples" (*Selections* 1: 57). To cite yet another example, in 1914 Du Bois again pointed to lust for Asian colonies as a cause of war (*Selections* 1: 83). Thus, to become involved in the word "Asia" is to become involved in a web of meaning that reveals domination, exploitation, war. In all cases, the Asians are blameless: they are lusted after, fought over, oppressed. It is Europe and America that kill in order to exploit. The allusive web of the word reveals America as something less than a land of the free and the brave.

Du Bois, however, did not stop at pointing to the colonial and imperial actions of Europe and America in Asia. He also connects the struggles of Asians to the struggles of African Americans. As part of a web of oppression that includes people of African descent, the struggles of the Asian people reveal to Du Bois a fundamental problem about the color line. As long as Europe and America oppress people of color elsewhere, people of color in America will not be free, because they, like their brothers and sisters elsewhere, are the dominated other.

Thus, Du Bois calls out for the freedom of Asia (and Africa). He links the struggles of African Americans with the struggles of other people of color. All suffer under European and American domination. All will be free together. One way to understand this connection that Du Bois was seeking is to consider an idea of his that arose late in his career at the *Crisis*. As a way to free both African Americans and people of color in Asia, Du Bois envisioned African American economic cooperatives that would avoid the American economic system. He understood this as indispensable to African American freedom and offered, with an allusive flourish, to include "all Asia" in these cooperative efforts. If successful, Du Bois thought that people of color will have "conquered a world" and that "no nation . . . can oppress us" (*Selections* 2: 694).

Du Bois's composition of the Orient as a homogeneous entity in order to challenge the color line extends beyond Asia, as the 1914 editorial titled "World War and the Color Line" reveals. Here, Du Bois composes Britain as a "blood-guilty" rapist of the "darker races," including India, which Britain starved (*Selections* 1: 84). Mixed metaphors aside (a rapist doesn't starve someone), Du Bois's point is clear.

In a 1919 piece titled "Forward," Du Bois reports that England sought the extradition of Hindus living in America working for the Indian liberation movement. Thus, by 1919, the pain of India is not simply "out there," a people of color battling a representative of the West; the pain is now internal to America: it rises within the country itself.

Du Bois discovered, as he states in a 1931 editorial titled "We Darker Ones," that India's suffering is not simply externally caused. At a meeting of "respectable, well-to-do white people in New York," Du Bois heard an Indian defend the caste system, which privileged the "white Brahmin" over the "black Sudra," as ideal. Du Bois reports that he was outraged, and he spoke against this system in the editorial itself, calling on the spirits of Tagore and Gandhi. These wise figures of the Orient, as will be discussed more fully below, challenge the Indian racist. This racist, Du Bois claims, is atypical. Tagore and Gandhi are the true representatives of the India Du Bois composes because they match his own desire to challenge the color line.

Du Bois's composition of India as a leader, if not *the* leader, of the struggle against the color line arose late in his editorship of the *Crisis.* Prior to 1931, India was most often composed as a suffering nation, struggling with other Oriental nations, among them Persia, Egypt, China, and Japan(see, for example, *Selections* 1: 18–27, 83, 356; 2: 461–62). As late as 1929, in fact, Du Bois saw only a glimmer of leadership in India, although a powerful glimmer. In "The Darker World" he envisions that "the power and leadership of yellow Asia is going to be able to challenge successfully the assumptions of white Europe" (*Selections* 2: 563). Specifically, Du Bois suggests that India (coupled with Russia) may be capable of leading this challenge, although this is not certain.

By the time of the 1931 editorial "Magnificent India," however,

Du Bois composes India as a leader of the worldwide revolution against European American domination. As the editorial shows, Du Bois calls on India "to reveal to the world the inner rottenness of European imperialism" (*Selections* 2: 609). America is allusively implicated in this because, as Du Bois reminds his readers time and time again in the pages of the *Crisis*, America too participates in the struggle over the lands occupied by people of color (see, for example, "The Wide Wide World," *Selections* 2: 461–62). As Du Bois writes in the 1919 editorial "The League of Nations," most people want "a swashbuckling anarchy, with a Jingo United States yelling in chorus with Jingoes of all Europe" (*Selections* 1: 246).

If, by 1931, Du Bois had composed India as a leader of people of color, he also looked to Japan and China for leadership. He wanted them to throw off European American domination, to stop their own war, and to unite with India in order to lead the worldwide struggle.

Echoing earlier editorials (for example, "World War and the Color Line," *Selections* 1: 83–85; "The World and Us," *Selections* 1: 328–30), the 1932 piece "Japan and China" composes the Sino-Japanese War as a complex global conflict involving not only China and Japan but America and Europe as well (*Selections* 2: 655). As Du Bois writes it, Japan seeks to make China "Asiatic" by seizing parts of the dismembered country (dismembered by European American domination) before Europe and America can stop it. China looks to Europe and America for help, and American propaganda tries to convince the American republic that Japan acts maliciously.

Du Bois, in order to counter the propaganda, writes the "real" story. While Japan's actions are not born of altruism, Europe and America would help China only for "the chance to make money," to exploit that country, as Japan knows. Du Bois composes a morass of violence caused by the will to oppress: Japan and the European American alliance want China; China looks to Europe and America despite the history of oppression; American propaganda deliberately misleads the public. At the end of the editorial, Du Bois offers little hope. The world lost its chance for peace when it chose not to disarm and pursue "the paths of peace" (*Selections* 2: 655). The Sino-Japanese War rages on.

Du Bois returns to China and Japan nearly a year later in his editorial titled "Listen, Japan and China" (*Selections* 2: 682). It opens with a thundering composition of these Orientals, calling on them to stop their fighting and assume the mantle of leadership: "Colossi of Asia and leaders of all colored mankind: for God's sake stop fighting and get together." Allusively composed as Colossi, and thus invested as one of the seven wonders of the world, China and Japan are implored to face two realities of the global situation. The first is that Europe and America are ruled by "blood-sucking, imperial tyrants" who gleefully watch the war, waiting for their chance to exploit both countries. The second reality is that the world of color still lacks leadership. The "twelve little black millions who live in the midst of western culture" are not in the position to lead. Thus Du Bois calls on China and Japan, divided by war, to unite. Significantly, India plays a part, albeit a passive one, in this composition. It awaits the call of a united China and Japan: "Beckon to the three hundred million Indians; drive Europe out of Asia."

By the time of this 1933 piece, gone is the composition of Japan as aggressor (see "The World and Us," *Selections* 1: 329). Du Bois simply recognizes that China and Japan are fighting and calls on them to discover a reasonable solution to the conflict.

The picture of Europe and America as greedy manipulators is also missing. Viewed through the experience of the Far East, especially that of China and Japan, the white world becomes, at best, parasitic and, at worst, demonic. Foreshadowing Malcolm X, Du Bois uses the term "blood-sucking" to describe the white world, thereby invoking mosquitoes, leeches, ticks, vampires. The vampire allusion seems the strongest given what follows in the editorial. Europe and America delight with "ghoulish glee" at the sight and smell of the "blood and smoke of Shanghai and Manchuria" (*Selections* 2: 682).

This editorial is a classic example of how foreign images, like China and Japan, are composed in order to address the color line in America itself. Du Bois writes of a situation far from America, far from an America deep in the Great Depression. It is this otherness, however, that provides him a place to look back into America itself and there compose a land ruled by vampires who oppress their own people of color while delighting in the suffering of others.

Whereas Du Bois understood the yellow people of the Orient and the black people of America as struggling along at the same point on parallel lines, lines that he intersected in his discourse so that the points of struggle could merge, King was born into a time when the Orient, and particularly Asia, so it seemed to him, had made greater strides. In the 1963 "Letter from Birmingham City Jail," King ironically notes that "the nations of Asia and Africa are moving with jetlike speed toward the goal of political independence, and we still creep at horse and buggy pace toward the gaining of a cup of coffee at a lunch counter" (292). King's point is this: in response to those white clergy who would have the movement slow down, King suggests that they consider the rapidity of liberation movements across the globe. With typical allusive movement, King does not spell these out for his audience. He simply presents the words and lets them analogically carry his argument: as the yellow people of Asia are to their countries, so should the blacks of America be to their country.

While King repeats this analogical move elsewhere (for example, the 1964 "Hammer on Civil Rights" 169–75), he also moves beyond analogy into identification. In the 1960 "The Burning Truth in the South," King claims that

[t]he arresting upsurge of Africa and Asia is remote neither in time nor in space to the Negro of the South. Indeed, the determination of Negro Americans to win freedom from all forms of oppression springs from the same deep longing that motivates oppressed peoples all over the world. (95–96)

More than an analogical connection, African Americans share with their compatriots in Asia a rootedness in the source of the longing for liberation. Separated by culture, by distance, they are not fundamentally separate at all. The liberation movements of Asia and America, both directed against white oppressors, arise from the same source.

Furthermore, in this same piece, Asia reveals to African Americans not only connectedness with the same source but also "the brotherhood of colonial colored men" (97). No longer simply sharing in the same source, Asians and African Americans have a familial connection: they are brothers united by the common experience of European American domination.

It is in moments like these that the King of the American holiday is an ironic figure of national adoration and celebration. This metaphor reveals, as well, a recasting of America. It is not the land of the free and the brave but a colonial power concerned to maintain the subjugation of its subjects.

King's use of Asia leads one to America as colonizer, America as the heir to its English parent. This, certainly, is not the normal web of meaning one finds within the word "America" as it is trumpeted in schools, in political speeches. At worst, as King suggests elsewhere, America has simply made some mistakes that it can correct if it is only true to its past. Here, however, King suggests that America is not what is normally considered America.

It is also important to note that this King is an early King. Often, critics contend that the late King was the more radical, more like Malcolm X. This, certainly, is true. By the time of his discussions about Vietnam, King became an American whom most would prefer to ignore. America, as a word, revealed webs of meaning wholly disconsonant with the self-righteous image that Americans often hold. However, this late King was not a shocking change. He is rooted in the early King and revealed throughout his work, including his allusive composition of the Orient.

The Orient, for Malcolm X, serves as a model of liberation as well as a potential ally of African Americans in their struggle against the color line in America. Thus, the alien other works in his discourse as a tool of critique: it serves to correct the American republic. A speech Malcolm X delivered on February 15, 1965—only one day after his house had been attacked with Molotov cocktails—demonstrates this. A portion reads:

> [O]ne of our first programs is to take our problem out of the civil rights context and place it at the international level, of human rights, so that the entire world can have a voice in our struggle. If we keep it at civil rights, then the only place we can turn for allies is within the domestic confines of America. But when you make it a human rights struggle, it becomes international, and then you can open the door

for all types of advice and support from our brothers in Africa, Latin America, Asia, and elsewhere. (*February* 104)

With typical allusiveness, Malcolm X places Asia alongside Africa and Latin America; for him, each term implies the other, each is a part of the others' webs of meaning. The reason for this is that Malcolm X understands that the people of these nations are, in terms of the revolution against European American domination, more advanced. As he says in many places, these people have been fighting since 1945 to overthrow their imperial oppressors (*Malcolm X Speaks* 50).

Moreover, Malcolm X looks, throughout his work, to the historic conference at Bandung. At times, he is not entirely certain when it occurred: "I think, 1954" (*Malcolm X Speaks* 5). However, it marks for him a monumental event: the global unification of people of color against European American oppression. The appeal to Bandung marks, without particular detail, with threads of allusive play, Malcolm X's attempt to link African Americans with people of color around the globe. The connection arises out of Malcolm X's awareness of Babel. He knows that there are different language communities, and he tries to create a global language, that of human rights, spoken by the majority of people around the globe. Thus, Asia leads to Africa, which leads to Latin America, which leads to Bandung, which leads to the United Nations, which leads back to the Organization of Afro-American Unity (OAAU) and the American republic.

In a speech at the founding rally of the OAAU, Malcolm X again discusses the need to transform the discourse of civil rights into the discourse of human rights. The OAAU has made this discourse shift its first priority and, importantly, has already received "promises of support . . . from many different independent nations in Africa, Asia, and Latin America" (*By Any Means* 57). Again, Asia stands with the nations of color, those that historically have suffered under European American domination. Malcolm X uses these nations (whichever they are) for two reasons. First, the allusive composition of these liberated people of color supports his attempt to transform the discourse of civil rights into that of human rights. These liberated countries, Malcolm X informs his audience, already have offered aid. Second, he invokes Asia (and Africa and Latin America) in order to move his audience to action: "Can we get your support for this project?" (57). Malcolm X composes Asia in order to bring America to account before the world at large. America, he believes, is incapable of self-judgment; it must be judged by others who can see more truly into the nature of the color line.

If Malcolm X composes Asia always with Africa and Latin America, allusively offering to his readers a triumvirate of people who are struggling valiantly against European American oppression, he has extraordinarily little to say about India as a member of the Orient. When India appears in Malcolm X's discourse, it appears in order to buttress his case for the internationalization of the African American movement. Following his hajj to Mecca, Malcolm X tells of being the state guest of Saudi Arabia. He frequented the "lobby of the Jedda Palace Hotel" because it afforded hem "sizable informal audiences of important men from many different countries." There, "an Indian official wept in his compassion for 'my brothers in your land.' " Instances like these reminded Malcolm X that African Americans are part of the "non-white peoples of the world" (*Autobiography* 346). India, thus, simply stands with Sudan, Ghana, Pakistan, Egypt, and the many other countries Malcolm composes: they mean to him a web of brotherhood.

So, Malcolm X was not ignorant of India, nor did he ignore it entirely. However, despite its enormous population, despite its place in the annals of revolution against European American domination, despite its prominent place in the rhetoric of Malcolm X's foil, King, neither the word nor the place served as a germinal point for Malcolm X. It simply sits as one part of the web of brotherhood Malcolm X finds in the allusive conjoined play of numbers of countries.

One can only conjecture why Malcolm X did not compose India as part of his effort to critique the color line. One possibility is that while India represents classic motifs—the internal lines of the caste system and the external line of imperialism—that Malcolm X usually found appealing, India also offered, on the surface at least, a successful embodiment of nonviolent response to the color line. By the time Malcolm X had begun his public career, Mahatma Gandhi and his followers had driven the British out of India. Malcolm X, were he to cite India positively, would have necessarily aligned himself with King and other African Americans who argued for the moral and pragmatic necessity of nonviolence. While Malcolm X did make overtures to the civil rights movement when he moved away from the Nation of Islam, he was not willing to embrace nonviolence.

The discussion that surrounds Malcolm X's composition of India in his autobiography is instructive here. Immediately before the composition, Malcolm X relates the story of one man in the Jedda Palace Hotel, a "cabinet minister from Black Africa." Having traveled through America, treated as a black man in a racist society, the minister's "eyes blazed in his passionate anger, his hands hacked the air: 'Why is the American black man so complacent about being trampled upon? Why doesn't the American black man *fight* to be a human being?' " (346).

While the *Autobiography* lets this narration pass without explanatory reflection, it serves to introduce the discussion of internationalism that follows. Particularly important in the quotation are two words, one that stands out, one that doesn't. The italicization of "fight" is not an act of whim. While the quotation marks indicate that Malcolm X is simply reporting what the minister said, this last sentence could have been left out.

However, Malcolm X wanted to report the exact feelings of an African brother, a member of an oppressed non-white people who, according to Malcolm X only four paragraphs later, are the most important people of color for African Americans (347). Africans, according to Malcolm X, believe that the African American movement is triply troubled. It has no goal. Its strategies are weak. It acts at the behest of "the white man." To correct itself, the movement should internationalize, linking itself in particular with African revolutionaries who, Malcolm X emphasizes, are incredulous that African Americans seem unwilling to "*fight.*" One can rest assured that neither Malcolm X nor the cabinet minister is referring to the fight of nonviolent resistance. This is emphasized with the verb Malcolm X attaches to the minister's hand motions as he speaks his anger: they *hack* the air. Thus, the minister's hands, as composed by the narrative, embody the violence of the minister's speech.

Wise Person

The Orient, for King, means more than Asia. It means, as well, India and that mysterious wise person of the Hollywood movie starring Ben Kingsley in the title role: Gandhi. While King composed India as a backward place that serves to critique America, he also composed it as the originary point of Gandhi.[1]

Whether it is to introduce a five-point reflection on nonviolence in the 1957 article "Nonviolence and Racial Justice" (King 7), to connect the student sit-in movement with the Indian struggle for independence in the 1961 address "Love, Law, and Civil Disobedience" (45), to think through the public implications of the Christian notion of love in the 1960 article "Pilgrimage to Nonviolence" (38), or to explain the difference between violence and nonviolence in the 1959 piece "The Social Organization of Nonviolence" (32), Gandhi serves King as an allusive marker of his own work.

Gandhi is allusive because King does not offer to his audiences a history of Gandhi's life and work. Rather, King simply "drops" Gandhi's name: "even by Gandhi," "I came upon the life and teaching of Mahatma Gandhi," and so on. Even when King elaborates his thought at length by way of Gandhi, the mahatma simply serves to help King along (see, for example, "An Experiment in Love" 16–20).

In this effort, King explains the ways in which the Montgomery bus boycott was infused by the "inspiration of Mahatma Gandhi" (16). Of the five points King makes in the article, he uses Gandhi explicitly to buttress two of them, the first and the fourth. Each time Gandhi serves authoritatively: "This is why Gandhi said," "Gandhi said," and "said Gandhi." The only introduction King provides to Gandhi is "the little brown saint of India" (17). King even says that "people who had never heard [of him] were now saying his name with an air of familiarity" (17). Gandhi, then, had come to serve as an allusive, authoritative marker, invoked by the protesters and by King in order to validate themselves. "Gandhi" brought with it a web of meaning that revealed to King, to his followers, and to the public a reason behind the methods of the protest.[2]

King's use of Gandhi dramatically makes evident one of Said's points concerning Orientalism. The very act of composition is an act of representation that is necessarily limited. The composition never reveals the entirety of that which is composed, primarily for two reasons. First, language can never capture a thing. Thus, even were he so inclined, King with his word "Gandhi" could simply never have put into discourse fully that "little brown saint." Second, King's ideology necessarily limited the way in which he composed Gandhi. He was not a Gandhian, if by that word one means a person who attempts to follow Gandhi strictly. Rather, King recognized—in Gandhi's philosophy of *satyagraha* and in his nonviolent resistance to British rule—experiences familiar to African Americans and civil rights workers. Working from his own tradition, he made human connections with the other and wrote it in order to emancipate African Americans. To read King's "Gandhi" is to read an allusive web of meaning that does not include all of Gandhi; it includes only those elements King found appropriate for the African American movement.

Du Bois, like King, found in India more than the suffering Orient, more than the possibility of liberation. India, for Du Bois, was the land of Gandhi and Tagore ("Magnificent India," *Selections* 2: 609). Gandhi is written as "an apostle of Peace, who means peace; and puts to shame the professional pacifist, who means less than nothing." Tagore is "the great poet, who gave up the bribe of an English knighthood." India, as sufferer, exists at the end of 150 years of English "tyranny" much as it did before: a country divided amongst its people, a division perpetuated by England in order to maintain power. India as leader is "magnificent," a potential example of racial and religious unity that offers to the world Gandhi, Tagore, and the vision of "Prince and Untouchable, Muslim and Hindu, all standing shoulder to shoulder."

It is significant that Du Bois composes both Gandhi and Tagore as representatives of India because together they speak more fully of their country than one alone could. Unlike King, who composed only Gandhi, Du Bois, ever the man of letters, composed both the mahatma and the poet.[3]

The "Magnificent India" editorial suggests that Du Bois read Gandhi in terms of the Western religious tradition. "Apostle of Peace," with "Peace" capitalized, alludes, it is reasonable to think, to the Christian tradition. The word "apostle" connects Gandhi to Jesus' disciples/

apostles who carried forward the "good news." While the content of this "good news" is still debated centuries after the crucifixion, one tradition understands Jesus to be the "Prince of Peace." Although Du Bois had abandoned traditional expressions of Christianity, he nevertheless often alluded to Jesus Christ, calling him the "Prince of Peace" (see, for example, "To the World," *Selections* 1: 318; "Peace on Earth," *Selections* 2: 436).[4] Thus, through this allusive play of words, Du Bois interweaves two webs of meaning.

Du Bois composed Gandhi in terms of the West in order to critique the West. First, he is offered by "Magnificent India" as the leader of passive resistance against tyranny. Thus, this figure who allusively stands in the Christian tradition works against so-called Christian countries. Second, Gandhi "puts to shame the professional pacifist." While Du Bois does not detail the phrase "professional pacifist" in this editorial, one needs only recall a 1913 editorial titled "Peace" (*Selections* 1: 57).

This editorial, written at the beginning of World War I, denounces American "peace societies." Du Bois writes, acidly, that the American peace movement "has been so dignified and aristocratic that it has been often most difficult for the humbler sort of folk to recognize it as the opponent of organized murder" (1: 57). To buttress this charge, Du Bois notes that the New York Peace Society applauded the war in the Balkans. Peace, the president of this society (or at least Du Bois's composition of the president of this society), claims, is only for those who deserve it.

In response, and as a foreshadowing of his composition of Gandhi as an "apostle of Peace," Du Bois claims that "Peace to-day, if it means anything, means the stopping of the slaughter of the weaker by the stronger in the name of Christianity and culture" (1: 57). Du Bois's point is clear. Those American peace societies that purportedly represent Christianity and culture fail both. Gandhi, as Du Bois suggests in "Magnificent India," written eighteen years later, embodies these elements. It is the alien, in Du Bois's composition, who wears the mantle of the West and in so doing brings shame upon the West itself.

Tagore, the great Indian man of letters, allows Du Bois to compose India as something other than Gandhian resistance to tyranny. Not only does India mean ascetic Hindus battling imperialism; it also means people at the pinnacle of culture engaged in the liberation movement. Tagore, as composed here, is especially important because he refused a British knighthood. Thus, Du Bois reveals, Tagore is great not only in the estimation of Du Bois; Britain itself, imperial ruler, recognized Tagore as such. Yet the acclaimed poet rejected the honors offered by his imperial masters. Like Gandhi, Tagore is composed to show that the West itself is rotten within: great men by the standards of the West reject it in favor of their own nation.

Backward Place

While Gandhi is an important part of King's composition of India, King also composes India without Gandhi. His composition of India reveals, in addition to Gandhi, both an oppressed people who are necessarily connected to African Americans and a source of ideas for the betterment of the American republic. While King does draw on classic American texts—the Declaration of Independence and so on—he also composes what is often understood to be other to America in order to address the republic's color line. India, for King, is more than Gandhi. It is, as well, this: a struggling people who both are in need of aid and can provide a place from which to criticize, and improve, America.

In a number of places, King recalls the trip that he made to India in 1959. In his first report, "My Trip to the Land of Gandhi," India is represented as a Gandhian land, "a tremendous force for peace and nonviolence," but also as deeply troubled by widespread poverty, a housing crisis, a food shortage, vast un- and underemployment, and segregation (23–30). King suggests, near the end of this piece, that "India needs help," that "it is in the interest of the United States and the West to help," and that they should do so with no strings attached (29). Such action, King argues, should be done not simply for diplomatic expedience; the United States and the West should act because it is the morally proper course (29).

In this piece King composes India as both superior and inferior to the United States; it is a source of critique and a place that needs help. On the one hand, it is the land of Gandhi, a force for peace and nonviolence. America can look to it, for instance, as model of a reconciled nation where "a mutual friendship based on complete equality exists between the Indian and British people within the commonwealth" (25).

On the other hand, India is wracked by social ills. King claims that India's housing crisis is greater than that of the United States' and that its food shortage is twice as serious as that of the United States' during the depression (27). The United States and the West, as India's other, need to help the country in order to insure the survival of democracy.

King returns to this trip in his 1961 commencement address, "The American Dream," but concentrates on composing India as suffering (208–16). In order to build his case that "we must all learn to live together as brothers, or we will perish together as fools" (209), King invokes the homeless and starving of Calcutta and Bombay and again calls on the United States to act. In his contemplation of the suffering in India, King realizes that America spends far too much money to store surplus food, far too much money to outfit its military. Because its destiny is part of India's, and vice versa, America should act to help India's homeless and starving masses (210).

King composes this same scene in his 1967 "A Christmas Sermon on Peace" (253–58). Again he finds fault with America's use of its resources, but he expands his call to aid beyond the suffering of India: he moves more globally to Asia, to Africa, to Latin America, and then, most pointedly, to America itself, where millions "go to bed hungry at night" (254). India, in this sermon near the end of King's life, serves as a suffering sibling who takes him back to America itself. Gone is the 1957, and even the 1961, King who saw America as a land of opulence. By 1967, America is both rich and poor: it needs to aid countries wracked by the history of the color line, but it needs as well to aid itself.

Given the contemporary debate over affirmative action policies in America, King's composition of India offers a final interesting challenge. In at least two pieces, his 1957 "My Trip to the Land of Gandhi" and his 1961 "Equality Now: The President Has the Power," King discovers affirmative action in India. Plagued by its caste system, and in particular the line that separated the "untouchables" from everybody else, India, King writes, decided to atone for "the injustices and indignities heaped in the past on their seventy million untouchable brothers" by setting aside for this class of people money for scholarships, financial grants, and the like ("Equality Now" 158). This composition of India is particularly pointed in the 1961 piece. Here, King tells the American government what steps it should take to correct the color line. The analogy hardly needed to be explained. America, like India, had created a class of untouchables. Unlike India, a dark country, a backward country, an other, America had yet to address the problems of the color line, had yet to rename the untouchables, as did Gandhi, "children of God" ("My Trip" 28).

For Malcolm X, the backwardness of the Orient, and the critical power thereby provided, is located most fully in the Far East, in particular China and Vietnam. In a 1965 speech, "Prospects for Freedom in 1965," Malcolm X composed China as an advanced nation that calls into question the intelligence of the American intellectual and political elite. Reviewing the progress of oppressed people in 1964, he notes that "China exploded her bomb" (*Malcolm X Speaks* 149). Malcolm X celebrates this achievement for two reasons. First, it makes evident that an oppressed people can gain power, and power is the "magic word" (150). Only power can fight power, and the bomb allowed China to meet the West as an equal.

Second, China's achievement calls into question American intelligence. He reminds his audience that "*this*" country (meaning America) keeps calling China "backward," "poor," and "so behind everybody" (149–50). Implicit is Malcolm X's belief that America has composed China incorrectly. China is not as backward as America would lead its people to believe. "Poor people can do it as well as rich people," Malcolm X writes.

For Malcolm X, the People's Republic of China served as a model of revolution and independent power. As a model of revolution, Malcolm X composes China as a warning to America. In his 1964 speech "The Harlem Hate-Gang Scare," Malcolm X foresees African Americans following the lead of other peoples of color around the globe, including China:

> The People of China grew tired of their oppressors and the people rose up against their oppressors. They didn't rise up nonviolently. It

was easy to say that the odds were against them, but eleven of them
started out and today those eleven control 800 million. They would
have been told back then that the odds were against them. As the
oppressor always points out to the oppressed, "The odds are against
you." (*Malcolm X Speaks* 68)

The Chinese revolution so composed is effortless. Unmentioned is
the long march, the years of savage fighting, the bloodshed, the bodies broken, the inevitable suffering that precedes the consolidation of
power in violent revolutions. Rather, Malcolm X simply cites the
"fact" that a small coterie of revolutionaries were able to overthrow
violently their oppressors, who outnumbered them greatly. The question of whether Malcolm X's vision of the revolution is true or not is
not the concern here, really. The point is this: his situation in America
led him to compose China in a way consonant with his own needs.
He ignores all but the vision of successful revolution. It is not even
particularly pertinent that the revolution was, in great part, a civil
war, Chinese against Chinese, people of color against people of color.

An earlier speech, "Message to the Grass Roots," which Malcolm
X delivered in 1963 not long before he left the Nation of Islam, does
compose the violence of the revolution, and lauds it. Reminding his
audience that true revolution is always about land, one of the dimensions of Babel discussed in chapter 2, Malcolm X narrates a story that
is a "good example." He tells of a little Chinese girl who shot her
father in the head during the revolution because he was "Uncle Tom
Chinaman." Her act simply represented the act of the whole population: all Uncle Tom Chinamen were killed. As a result, China is "one
of the toughest, roughest, most feared countries on this earth—by the
white man. Because there are no Uncle Toms over there" (*Malcolm X
Speaks* 8).

Thus composed, China is a place of violent power unleashed in
order to cleanse itself of internal discrepancy, in order to purify the
nation. Prior to the revolution, some Chinese identified with the oppressive regime, similar to the way in which Malcolm X's "house
Nigger" identified with the white master. China, bold, violent, strong
China, simply acted as an oppressed daughter should. America might
see China as backward, but China, Malcolm X declares, is an example of revolutionary power.

It is instructive at this point to consider King's countercomposition of China in order to highlight a fundamental difference—beyond the question of nonviolence—between King and Malcolm X. King, by 1966, publicly opposed the compositions of China offered by Malcolm X (and Du Bois for that matter). In his "Nonviolence: The Only Road to Freedom," he scoffs at the idea that there is a worldwide movement of people of color that in righteous unity will rise up to "throw off the yoke of white oppression" (55–56). He doesn't dislike the idea; he simply thinks it is irrelevant because it is so distant. As will be discussed in chapter 4, King composes African nations as almost hopelessly torn by internal problems and neocolonialism. China he simply dismisses out-of-hand (56).

Two years later, in fact, King composes China as a specter of the possibility of nuclear war. In his 1967 "Remaining Awake Through a Great Revolution," King discusses the war in Vietnam and, because China stands behind Vietnam, the possibility of war with China. King fears that if America does not end its campaign in Vietnam, it will "inevitably come to the point of confronting China which could lead the whole world to nuclear annihilation." Such a scene, King claims with typically allusive adroitness, would be "an inferno that even the mind of Dante could not imagine" (276). Unlike Malcolm X, who composed backward China as a model nation because of its nuclear capacity, King writes China as a nuclear other to be avoided: China means the potential end of the world.

Malcolm X also composes Vietnam as a backward place that challenges American criminal behavior. To return again to his 1965 speech "Prospects for Freedom in 1965," one finds there a joyful celebration of the Vietnam War. Malcolm X composes the Vietnamese revolutionaries both as underestimated warriors in an oppositional relationship with Goliath and as characters in a children's nursery rhyme.

As warriors, the "little rice farmers, peasants" armed only with "a rifle," have withstood the onslaught of "jets, napalm, battleships, everything else" (*Malcolm X Speaks* 148). The match is unevenly ironic. It looks as if the "little rice farmers, peasants" should lose, but in fact they are winning. Malcolm X's choice of nouns and adjectives—little rice farmers, peasants—only heightens the distinction he draws here.

At first glance, the terms are disparaging: they are stereotypical representations of the Oriental. Yet, they only bring into greater relief the achievements Malcolm X celebrates: these little folk are winning the battle against the gargantuan, technological forces of America.

Most fascinating in this celebration of the war is Malcolm X's allusive play with a children's nursery rhyme, Humpty Dumpty. This play reveals Malcolm X's cutting humor. He uses a standard part of the education of young Americans, arising as it does out of the white tradition, in order to make fun of the American failure in Vietnam. While the little rice farmers stand as mighty warriors, the Americans are characters in a nursery rhyme, characters who failed at their appointed task. The egg is broken and America can do nothing to put it back together.

That America is involved at all in this effort to mend the broken egg is stupid and criminal. Malcolm X does not stop at composing white America as the characters of a nursery rhyme. In the same speech he declares that the American action in Vietnam is "criminal," for two reasons: America deceives its public in order to carry out the war, and it sends its "soldiers to be murdered every day, killed every day, die every day, for no reason at all" (*Malcolm X Speaks* 149).

To highlight even more fully the relationship between Malcolm X and King, it is instructive to turn to King's own composition of Vietnam. It has, certainly, been discussed in detail elsewhere, most notably by Cone (235–43). Important for this particular book, however, is a fascinating comment King makes about Ho Chi Minh and his followers. It is part of what Cone calls "King's great 'Beyond Vietnam' " speech—"A Time to Break Silence"—delivered at Riverside Church in 1967, one year before his assassination. After discussing the link between the war and the color line in America, King writes that the Vietnamese people

> must see Americans as strange liberators. The Vietnamese people proclaimed their own independence in 1945 after a combined French and Japanese occupation, and before the Communist revolution in China. They were led by Ho Chi Minh. Even though they quoted the American Declaration of Independence in their own document of

freedom, we refused to recognize them. Instead, we decided to support France in its reconquest of her former colony. (235)

This quotation is significant because King brings to his audience's attention both the global power of one of the founding documents of the American republic and the American republic's inability, or unwillingness, to listen to the call of its own emancipatory composition. As King composes them, the North Vietnamese—whom many Americans saw as the commie gooks, the slant-eyes, the devils—had actually turned to the American tradition in order to validate their struggle for independence against colonialism. A document produced by white European Americans, King writes, spoke to the condition of an Oriental people of color.

However, America did not heed this call to its own past. Rather, it aligned itself with a European imperialist and eventually took the place of that imperialist. Thus, America came to fight against itself: the people it battled understood themselves to be following the American tradition of anticolonial liberation. In so battling itself, America deepened the problem of the color line. In order to wage war against a foreign people of color who quoted the Declaration of Independence, America kept its own people of color oppressed. Vietnam allows King to compose America as a country deaf to its own emancipatory tradition, deaf to its own words that call for the overthrow of oppressive tyrants, words that demand liberty and justice for all.

4 | Africa

> [Aunt Fannie's] idea of Africa is a hair-raising blend of
> lore and hearsay and imagination. She thinks of it with
> nostalgia and longing—a kind of earthly Other Shore,
> Eden and Heaven—and yet she fears it because of its
> presumed darkness, its endless jungles, its stock of
> deliberately malevolent serpents and man-eating beasts.
> —Wendell Berry, *The Hidden Wound*

This book's discussion of "Africa," like that of the "Orient," might confound conservatives and extremists alike. Those on the so-called Right, the conservatives, might wonder why American students need know this term and its web of associations. What does Africa have to do with American education, American knowledge, American literacy? Those on the so-called Left, the extremists, might be perplexed as well. They might wonder why I, who profess parochially American inclinations, who is a conservative, would include this term, would demand that Americans who would be literate know Africa and its web of associations. Africa, after all, necessarily leads to a condemnation of the American republic. To consider this word's web of meanings leads one to consider, sooner or later, the slave trade that affected profoundly the development of Europe, of America, and of Africa itself.

However, Africa does not lend itself to the easy opposition that characterizes Orient/Occident or West/East. While Europe/Africa and America/Africa are certainly important dialectical pairs, they simply do not, at least as of 1999, carry the same urgency as Orient/Occident and East/West. They do not skip lightly off the tongue. They are not commonplace. This is despite the fact that Africa is central to America.

This may be because "Africa," as Christopher Miller argues, "has no positive shape of its own." Because the Occident/Orient (or, as

Miller says, Europe/Orient) dialectic is dominant, Africa "tends to be associated with one side or the other or to be nullified by the lack of an available slot in our intellectual apparatus" (16). This chapter will not be a discussion of Africa as what Miller calls a "natural object" (xi), if there even is such a thing. Miller seems to suggest that there is both a linguistic Africa and a natural Africa, but this is doubtful. The somatic elements that compose what we call Africa are, after all, known through language; Africa is a word. Thus, it is finally impossible to distinguish Africa as a natural object and Africa as a linguistic object. Africa is necessarily involved in the web of language.

In any case, Du Bois—in the February 1916 editorial titled "That Capital 'N' " (*Selections* 1: 117)—helpfully illuminates the dilemma that Miller discusses. Du Bois opens the piece with this explanation for its existence: "From time to time persons write us for a brief statement for the reasons for capitalizing the word *Negro*." Noting that the standard rules of grammar "enjoin the use of a capital letter for all proper nouns," Du Bois holds that "Negro" was, in fact, capitalized until "late in the Nineteenth Century," since it does refer "to a race of men." With the late nineteenth century, however, came the formal defense of slavery, a defense that composed "Negroes" as less than human. African Americans came to be written as either "'real estate' " or "property like horses, cows, etc."

Du Bois brings into relief the violent tension at the heart of America. The struggle over the capitalization of the word "Negro" was not simply a lexical struggle, above and beyond the oppression of slavery that marked America throughout most of the nineteenth century. Rather, the struggle over the capitalization of the word "Negro," as a struggle of literacy, interpenetrates the violent treatment visited upon the minds and bodies of slaves delivered to America, slaves no longer referred to by their original tribal names, slaves now called "Negroes" or, as the defenders of slavery would have it, "negroes."

Du Bois goes on in this editorial to write that simultaneous to the racist defense of slavery, printers began to claim that "Negro" referred not to a race of people but rather to color. Thus "Negro," like other colors, was to remain uncapitalized. Du Bois vociferously rejects these arguments and offers a counter in the final paragraph of the editorial:

This argument is manifestly false. Black is the correlative of white and Negro does not describe color since all the persons designated as Negroes are by no means black, even in Africa. If, therefore, we follow analogy we cannot refuse to capitalize Negro when we capitalize Caucasian, Malay, Indian, Chinese, etc. Not to capitalize Negro under such circumstances is a direct, and in these days a more and more conscious, insult to at least 150,000,000 human beings and no person or institution will persist in this insult if they realize that these people regard the usage as such. (*Selections* 1: 117)

The web of meaning involved in the word "Negro" brings us to the history of the battle over its capitalization as well as to the battle over the composition of Africa. As the final paragraph in Du Bois's editorial makes clear, the struggle over the capitalization of "Negro" is not simply a struggle over this word. It is, as well, a struggle over the composition of all members of the African diaspora—most notably African Americans—and Africa itself.

Du Bois claims that "Negro," despite its apparent connection to the Spanish language, does not mean black. Rather, it refers to the indigenous peoples of sub-Sahara Africa. Thus, "Negro" means Africans of varying shades, not simply black. The printer's lowercase *n*, ostensibly done for lexical reasons, actually perpetuates racism because it identifies heterogeneous peoples as unified on account of color.

Given Du Bois's treatment of "Negro" as a site of struggle, one must call into question a contention central to E. D. Hirsch's take on cultural literacy: "There is no point in arguing about . . . our vocabulary," he holds, because "our national vocabulary" is "an instrument of communication among diverse cultures rather than a cultural or class instrument in its own right" (103–4). This claim, it seems reasonable to argue with the help of Du Bois, simply isn't correct. Du Bois reveals that the national vocabulary *is* a site of contention, used to compose places and people in a way to benefit slavery and racism. The vocabulary of a nation is a site of argument. This is certainly true of the word "Africa," as Christopher Miller holds.[1]

Miller argues that Africa is filled in one of two ways: "Throughout the history of Africanist writing there is a striking tendency toward dual, polarized evaluations . . . Africa has been made to bear a double burden, of monstrousness and nobility" (5). Miller, for his part, concentrates on the literary productions of France and England in order to explore this, searching the pages of such authors as Céline and Conrad. His point, however, is true of American culture, "pop" and elite.

Consider, for instance, an English composition student in the Summer Bridge Program at the University of Illinois at Chicago. Designed primarily for people of color who were to enter school as freshmen, the Bridge Program served an extraordinary range of students, nearly all Latino and African American. One in particular stands out. Raised in the African American ghettos of Chicago's west side, he was reared by his mother and had, for all intents and purposes, no father. Most often, he wore dark shorts and T-shirts—basic clothes. A terrible student, both in terms of work habits and product, he was a standard graduate of Chicago's inner-city public schools.

However, his classmates afforded him an elevated status. They all recognized that he was a terrible student, but two facts elevated him: he wore a black and red leather icon of Africa around his neck, and he was studying to become a Muslim. The poor, ghetto-born and -raised, Africa-bearing Muslim-to-be excited, thrilled, perhaps even scared the other students in the class.

The black and red leather icon of Africa that he wore on his chest was clearly a rhetorical strategy. Rather than walking the streets of Chicago and the halls of the university preaching the power of the homeland, this student publicly composed Africa on his own body: one only had to look at him to see his message.

Unlike Hester Prynne's scarlet A, the icon was self-imposed and was worn as a badge of honor, as a defiant gesture meant to demonize America and sanctify Africa. He viewed Africa as his homeland, as the homeland of all African Americans, and he wanted the public to know it. As a child of the ghetto, he felt marginalized from the European American social structures that dominate America and chose to respond with the proclamation of Africa. Had that composition classroom been more fully centered around the idea of emancipatory composition, that student's icon could have served as a perfect entrée into potentially powerful student writing.

Of course, the danger of consumer America is that the icon of Africa often simply stands as an aestheticized piece of jewelry, the chic product of New York and Paris runways or a cheap "knock-off" sold in discount stores. Only if Africa is part of one's literacy, part of one's worldview—either a positive or negative part—can the icon be understood as a response to the color line in America.

This student's stand opposes the American composition of Africa as savage, threatening, inferior, monstrous even. In the very childhood air that many breathe floats the image of Africa as the land of "spooks" and "monkeys." America's composition of Africa as savage, as monstrous, is so commonplace that it hardly needs elucidation. Slavery was justified, in part, by the claim that Africans were in need of the civilizing character of European American culture. So too missionary activity to Africa was justified, in part, by the claim that Africa was a dark land in need of the salvific light of the gospel of Jesus Christ.

The film *Legends of the Fall* is a wonderful example of the American double composition of Africa as noble and monstrous. *Legends of the Fall* is worthy of further consideration for one primary reason: as a film it speaks to an extraordinary number and range of Americans. It has an audience that more "traditional" composition—spoken or written—can only dream of. As a film, it is a popular device and thus reveals not simply the interests of an American academic but also the interests of the American citizenry, broadly cast. Granted, many may pay to see the film primarily because they are fans of the actors involved. Current heartthrob Brad Pitt, for instance, attracted many thirteen-year-old girls to the film. They did not see it in order to explore Africa, but nonetheless Africa was given to them. "Africa" is not simply the favored icon of radical Afrocentric college students and professors; it is part of the lives of all Americans.

The movie presents the following African dynamic. Tristan, the prodigal son, leaves the ranch his father has dedicated to racial harmony. In Africa, Tristan finds animals he has never seen before, animals he kills as "the great white hunter." In a scene crucial to the film's double composition of Africa as both savage and noble, Tristan witnesses a black African removing the heart of a beast that he, the African, has just killed. The African holds the heart high, as Tristan himself was taught to do with the heart of a kill by his Cherokee teacher. This is necessary, one learns earlier in the film, in order to set free the animal's spirit.

Thus, Africa is doubly composed. At one level, it is the land of the savage. The almost-naked African squats to cut open the kill, rips the heart from the still-warm body, and holds it high and red for all to see. Such action is considered uncivilized in modern European America. At another level, however, this scene composes black Africa as noble. Away from the ranch and the madness of European American civilization, Tristan, the film's tormented but noble protagonist, discovers a link between himself and the African, a link provided by the Cherokee mentor. While the film indulges in stereotypes (for example, Tristan as the great white hunter surrounded by primitive black Africans in loincloths), it does so as a way to explore the color line in America. Tristan is offered as a symbol of the European American trying to compose Africa as noble self, not as savage other.

So too *School Daze*, the second feature film directed by the African American artist Spike Lee, composes Africa doubly. A musical exploration of racial/political tensions at a historically African American college in the South, *School Daze* presents to its audience a fundamental opposition, the organizing nucleus of which is Africa. At one pole are the members of a fraternity, dedicated to assimilation and financial success in white America. On the other side are young radicals who reject the impulses that motivate the fraternity, who wear African clothing, and who protest apartheid in South Africa. Each rejects the other just as vehemently as the KKK might reject Malcolm X.

At the center of the groups' opposition is Africa itself. The fraternity brothers proclaim that they are Americans. The leader, in a memorable conflict with the leader of the radical faction, consciously identifies himself with Detroit: the civilized city of cars is his homeland. In contrast, the radicals, and in particular their leader, identify not with America but with Africa. They wear elements of African clothing; their leader is consumed not by his schoolwork, not by his attempt to find success in America, but with the liberation struggles of African peoples. Thus, *School Daze* is Lee's attempt to explore the dynamics of Africa and the color line in America through a unique prism. Rather than staging a struggle between "whites" and "blacks," he stages a struggle between opposing African Americans who compose Africa differently.

While Christopher Miller's appraisal of the composition of Africa as noble and monstrous is important, it is also limited. In the American republic, another composition is just as strong: Africa as the suffering other in need of assistance. One need only flip through the pages of a general-readership magazine or watch television to find this composition. Charitable organizations like World Vision and Save the Children present to American audiences a never-ending stream of suffering black African children who need "you," the viewer, to send only ten cents per day. For instance, contributors to Save the Children receive special appeals like this one: "Every $10 you give can help provide a day's emergency rations of grain and oil for 150 African children on the edge of starvation." Accompanying this written text was a visual one that depicts a black African child obviously suffering the effects of malnutrition.

UNICEF also composes Africa as the suffering other. At a UNICEF Halloween party, complete with a dinner of abundant pizza, guests were asked to donate money to the children's fund. As a persuasive technique, the organizers of the party showed a UNICEF video, which depicted malnourished black African children listlessly wandering on the screen. The point could not have been more obvious.

Du Bois, King, and Malcolm X, as they compose Africa in order to emancipate America, are part of the American mainstream, providing further proof that "Africa" is part of American literacy. Each composes Africa so that this term, internal to the constitution of American culture, reveals the disease at the center of the republic: the color line. They compose Africa within the categories described above—suffering and monstrousness/nobility—but do so in order to critique and emancipate America itself.[2]

Africa as Suffering

As early as 1913, Du Bois composed Africa as a site of suffering. In the May 1913 editorial titled "Peace," he obliquely composes Africa oppressed: "The modern lust for land and slaves in Africa, Asia, and the South Seas is the greatest and almost the only cause of war between the so-called civilized peoples" (*Selections* 1: 57).

Here, Africa as a site of suffering is composed with both a passive and active value. Passively, as an equal of Asia and the South Seas, it is the cause of the coming war. It stands as a mine of natural and human resources that other nations take, over which other nations fight. Africa itself is not an actor in the coming conflagration; it is only acted upon.

Actively, Africa (and these other lands) helps Du Bois define the West. As theorists from Saussure on remind their students, terms have meaning only relative to their play with and against other terms. Thus, one knows dog only relative to cat, man only relative to woman, and the like. This, certainly, is one of Christopher Miller's points in his study of Africanist discourse: Europe offers definitions of Africa over and against which it can define itself. Here, Du Bois engages in this dialectical definitional play for the benefit of a mass readership. As a passive mine of natural and human resources, Africa serves actively as a foil against which the true nature of the "so-called civilized peoples" is revealed. In their lust for slaves and land, these nations, nations of the West, reveal themselves as something other than civilized. America is indicted, at least in this editorial, because its "peace movements" care little about "this problem of machine guns, natives and rubber" (*Selections* 1: 57). America, represented by its peace organizations, participates in the mining of these nations. Thus, it too is a "so-called civilized" nation.

While Du Bois often composes Africa in general as a site of suffering in order to reveal the true nature of the West in general and America in particular, his most powerful compositions are those dealing with specific African locales, such as Rhodesia. Speaking of his beloved England in a 1920 editorial, Du Bois connects England, America, Negro, Rhodesia, and Africa in order to condemn England explicitly and America implicitly (*Selections* 1: 251–52). The editorial opens with this bold sentence: "I was reared in an atmosphere of admiration—almost veneration—for England." Du Bois goes on to tell (or remind) his readers that "the New England of my birth and day was English in its soul." Indeed, its language, its history, its system of governance were English. Du Bois, as an American born and raised in Massachusetts, is also a child of New England and, thus, given the era in which he lived, a child of England as well. By the end of the first paragraph, Du Bois has revealed a metonymic web of meaning involving three terms that interpenetrate each other: America/New England/England.

Moreover, Du Bois the American/New Englishman is connected to England by more than birth and rearing: as an adult he has "visited England four times and met and known many Englishmen." These encounters left him with a sense of admiration for both the "Englishman of birth and breeding" and, strangely, "the Empire on which the sun never set."

By the end of the second paragraph of this editorial, then, Du Bois establishes himself as deeply connected to England. By birth and rearing, by adult experience, he is deeply endowed with a sense of being partially an Englishman. He makes this connection, one soon discovers, in order to advance his editorial dialectically.

The third paragraph, in contrast to the first two, reveals to the reader the moment when Du Bois's love of things English came into question: he witnessed, in Glasgow, a police officer beating a prostitute. While, as he says, "Glasgow is not England and the East End is not London," he came to doubt England nonetheless. The allusive relationship between the Glasgow prostitute and the "Englishman of birth and breeding" was too strong. Scotland's relationship to England, although Du Bois never says this explicitly, is only too clear.

In a masterful demonstration of emancipatory composition, Du Bois sees in the body of the Glasgow prostitute the English empire itself, an empire organized and administered by that "Englishman of birth and breeding." While the police officer might be a Scot, he represents England. Thus, while he beats the young woman, England beats her, as well.

This insight allows Du Bois to make the following connections:

[T]here comes to me from English sources this terrible tale of theft, murder, and outrage done by Englishmen to Negroes, unrebuked by English government and unprotested for a generation. English missionaries long ago entered the land of the Matabele and Mashona peoples, in the Zambese basin. An English company in 1889 was allowed to enter, on the express condition that it regard native law and land rights. Yet today 800,000 Negroes of this country, now called Rhodesia, have absolutely no title to 90 million acres of their own land! As Englishmen themselves write: "The land rights of the natives have been appropriated simply by fraud and theft—that is the beginning and end of the whole sordid story." (*Selections* 1: 251–52)

Rhodesia is not simply Rhodesia; it represents both Africa (the next sentence begins "If we turn from Africa to Asia") and Negroes in general (Du Bois claims this is outrage against Negroes, not Rhodesians). Thus, Du Bois, the American/New Englishman/Englishman, confronts, through an allusive web of meaning, Africa as oppressed. He sees the suffering because he, as an American/New Englishman/Englishman, saw it in Glasgow. The importance of the editorial in which he discusses the capitalization of "Negro" cannot be emphasized enough here. This is what connects him, as an African American, to Africa by way of Rhodesia, to Rhodesia by way of Africa.

Not to be overlooked are two important facets of the quotation above. First, Du Bois uses the words of Englishmen, at the end of the quotation, to condemn England and all who would identify with her. He doesn't need to criticize the imperial order from the outside because people from within are doing this work. Second, "Africa" is not the trope that it is in other editorials, a site of vague suffering. As he concentrates on a specific locale, he finds specific detail—the numbers of black Rhodesians suffering, the amount of land stolen.

Some may be troubled at this point by a nagging suspicion. As Said suggests in regard to the Orient in the compositions of Orientalists, the other—in this case Africa—is often written not as an end but as a cause. In Said's own words, "He is never concerned with the Orient except as the first cause of what he says." Said goes on to argue that this strategy is a way to demarcate oneself from the other: "What he says and writes, by virtue of the fact that it is said or written, is meant to indicate that the Orientalist is outside the Orient, both as an existential and as a moral fact" (20–21).

Given Said's reasoning, it might be possible to level a criticism against Du Bois, Malcolm X, and King. They compose Africa as suffering not to plead the case for Africa but as way to plead the case for African Americans. Without doubt, Du Bois, King, and Malcolm X do not offer sustained engagement with Africa. They do not offer detailed, lengthy analysis of the problems that beset "Africa." Rather, they compose Africa in snippets, in fragmentary moments.

Paul Gilroy's discussion of Du Bois's novel *Dark Princess* offers a way to consider the works of Du Bois, King, and Malcolm X relative to this problem that Said highlights. Concerning the conclusion of Du Bois's novel, Gilroy offers this provocative thought:

> [I]t offers an image of hybridity and intermixture that is especially valuable because it gives no ground to the suggestion that cultural fusion involves betrayal, loss, corruption, or dilution. . . . This is not the fusion of two purified essences but rather a meeting of two heterogeneous multiplicities that in yielding themselves up to each other create something durable and entirely appropriate to troubled anticolonial times. (144)

While Du Bois's, King's, and Malcolm X's compositions of Africa—and the Orient—are fragmentary and allusive, their compositions, nonetheless, attempt to join, as Gilroy would have it, "heterogeneous multiplicities." Thus, the three do not simply struggle with the Orient or with one dimension of the Orient. Rather, they struggle with the multiple manifestations of the Orient and various meanings suggested by these terms. So too Africa becomes "Africa" meant heterogeneously. It is not just Africa, but Rhodesia and, as I will discuss shortly relative to Malcolm X, the Congo and other elements that compose what has come to be called Africa.

Moreover, as was discussed above, Du Bois's composition of Africa leads him and his readers not only beyond Africa into Rhodesia but also back into England, into New England, into America, into Du Bois's own self. There he finds heterogeneous facets. England is, at once, beloved and detested, and, by implication, Du Bois calls his own self into question. Given his respect for the empire, his encounter with the evil of colonialism in Glasgow and Rhodesia leads him to an encounter with his own dialectical problematic: the empire, deep inside himself, is both attractive and repulsive. This play is the ultimate possibility of mature emancipatory composition. One becomes intimately involved in the webs of meaning that words represent and, in so doing, discovers links, connections, trails unimagined.

So too in King's composition of Africa as a site of suffering, one discovers King using the word not only to critique the West in general and America in particular but also as an entry into a global world of complex connections among heterogeneous people and cultures. In fact, King rarely, if ever, composes Africa as a site of suffering alone. Unlike his compositions of India, King writes suffering Africa as a member of the globally oppressed, a key part of the seemingly heterogeneous peoples who, in fact, share something in common— European American domination.

Speaking of poverty as a global "challenge" that is "closely related to racism," King declares in his 1968 sermon "Remaining Awake Through a Great Revolution" that

> [l]ike a monstrous octopus, poverty spreads its nagging, prehensile tentacles into hamlets and villages all over our world. They are ill-housed, they are ill-nourished, they are shabbily clad. I have seen it in Latin America; I have seen it in Africa; I have seen this poverty in Asia. (271–72)

Africa thus composed comprises people suffering from lack of food, shelter, clothing. Africa thus composed is a member of the suffering family of nations, of continents of color that have undergone European American oppression. Rather than delving into each of these areas individually, King continues on in the speech to delve specifically, once again with a familiar story, into India. He tells of the suffering he and Mrs. King saw there. Africa, in this speech, is written as a site of suffering. King simultaneously proposes that poverty is a heterogeneous and homogeneous global experience. He knows that it occurs in different cultures—America, Africa, Latin America, Asia. He also suggests it has the same characteristics wherever it is found and that India, at least the India he and Mrs. King came to know, can analogously illuminate the global experience of poverty.

King uses this list of suffering countries of color in order to reread America itself. Following a plea to divert monies spent for military purposes into antipoverty programs for foreign countries, King moves back to America itself as a cradle of poverty: "I would remind you that in our own nation there are about forty million people who are poverty-stricken. . . . I have seen them in the ghettos of the North; I have seen them in the rural areas of the South" (272). While he doesn't immediately specify that he is speaking about African Americans, it soon becomes clear that he is: his examples are "little black boys and black girls" and "welfare mothers" in "Newark and Harlem."

Consider, as well, his 1967 "A Time to Break Silence," best known as the speech in which he declared clearly his opposition to the Vietnam War. In the speech, he again returns to the issue of poverty and also to the ways in which capitalist economic practices are indicted in the globalization of poverty.

> A true revolution of values will soon look uneasily on the glaring contrast of poverty and wealth. With righteous indignation, it will look across the seas and see individual capitalists of the West investing huge sums of money in Asia, Africa and South America, only to take the profits out with no concern for the social betterment of the countries, and say: "This is not just." (241)

One could, as a criticism of King, claim that here he raises, once again, the usual litany of oppressed: Asia, Africa, Latin America. One could, as a critical question, ask why King attends to the specifics of India and Vietnam but not of Africa. After all, in this very same speech, as I discussed in chapter 2, King discusses Ho Chi Minh, the Vietnamese appeal to the American Declaration of Independence, and the history of French colonialism in Vietnam. Of course, this speech is about Vietnam. Nonetheless, it is important to wonder why King, unlike Du Bois and Malcolm X, foregoes specific attention to the sufferings of Africa.

Though no definitive answer to this question is possible, there are two possibilities. First, King was connected to India through his commitment to nonviolent social change. Thus, it was inevitable that India would have a central place in his compositions. Second, Vietnam came to possess America in the 1960s in a way that the struggles for independence in Africa simply did not. As an American, King came to face this question in a way he simply did not have to about the specificities of suffering in Africa.

Yet, the ramifications of his composition of Africa as a member of this list of suffering lands is clear and powerful. King cannot, it seems, compose Africa without this word revealing to him, and thus his audiences, the global network it means. Africa's web of meaning, as King tends to compose it, is not simply that of the continent we now call Africa nor of Africans in the diaspora. Rather, Africa also means a site of suffering; it means people of color who suffer.

Moreover, this speech reveals, as Cone maintains, how radical the late King had become. This is not the iconized King of the "I Have a Dream" speech. This is a King closer to Malcolm X than stereotypical understandings of King would lead one to believe possible. This is a King who finds ironic the fact that America rejects, in favor of French colonial aspirations, Vietnamese liberation fighters who quote the Declaration of Independence.

This is not to say that King here is no longer that figure upheld as what is good about America, as an exemplar American. King does believe that he is working to bring to fruition the fundamental aspirations of the American republic. However, King has also come to call into question the basic economic practice of the United States and, thus, the United States itself. As he saw Africa, along with others, suffering, he saw that capitalism abetted, even caused, this suffering. While he rejects communism as well, King by the end of his life found in Africa and other nations a bloody condemnation of the economic order of the republic itself. Were one to study King's play with "capitalism," one would find within this word's web of meaning another word—unjust.

Whereas King composed Africa as a site of suffering, Malcolm X tended to compose as suffering particular fragments of Africa, most notably the Congo. This is not to say that Malcolm X did not write the suffering of Africa. Even a quick glance at his speech titled "The Black Revolution" shows that he, like King, brought Africa to America as the suffering other that is not as other as one might first imagine. Consider, for instance, this sentence:

> I think that nobody would disagree that the dark masses of Africa and
> Asia and Latin America are already seething with bitterness, animos-
> ity, hostility, unrest, and impatience with the racial intolerance that
> they themselves have experienced at the hands of the white West.
> (*Malcolm X Speaks* 47)

The surface of this sentence reveals Malcolm X's interpretation of
the psychological state of "the dark masses" around the globe. Yet, as
Malcolm X states with some reserve at the end, this psychological
unrest has been caused by "racial intolerance." The "white West," in
short, has caused them to suffer.

Like King, Malcolm X speaks of Africa here as member of a globally oppressed group, suggesting to his readers that Africa reveals in
its web of meaning other entities. Africa cannot be considered alone;
it does not suffer uniquely. Malcolm X reinforces this point later in
the speech when he claims that "[w]hat happens to a black man in
America today happens to the black man in Africa. What happens to
a black man in America and Africa happens to the black man in Asia
and to the man down in Latin America" (48). Again, Malcolm X is
relatively subdued here, speaking of suffering in vague terms like
"what happens." That "what happens" refers to suffering can be
known in the context of the speech. The paragraph preceding it
speaks of "racial violence and much racial bloodshed." Following is
Malcolm X's claim that when the "whites . . . touch this one, they are
touching all of them." The touch, it is clear, is not a caress; it is, rather,
the touch the Cleveland police shared with "our people"—water hoses
and tear gas (49). While Malcolm X acknowledges that "our people"
responded with physical violence, he implies that the police began
the confrontation. "Our people" became "the victim of brutality."

Important to note is the metaphoric move Malcolm X accom-
plishes in this speech, a move that draws all people of color under the
aegis of black Africa. While the suffering of Africa in this speech is a
suffering alongside other spaces of color, the other spaces of color
are, in fact, black African. The suffering of black Africa serves as an
Ur-category for Malcolm X.

However, he knows that suffering is heterogeneous. As he says
later in the speech, "[W]hen I say black, I mean non-white—black,
brown, red, or yellow." As Gilroy suggests relative to Du Bois, Mal-

colm X tries to balance his homogenizing tendencies with his recognition of the heterogeneity of suffering people of color. Malcolm X knows that they aren't all black. Thus, he finds it appropriate, even necessary, to step away from his discourse, to interrupt it with a moment of theoretical reflection on the word "black."

It is easy to conjure two reasons for this. First, it could be the effect of having believed fervently in the myth of racial history proffered by the Nation of Islam. He explains it in the speech titled "Black Man's History," delivered in 1963 at the end of his time with the Nation (*End* 23–66). According to this myth, black men were the originary humans, and all other colors of people were derived from blacks (55–56). Second, and this seems to be the most reasonable idea, Malcolm X simply wrote these suffering others according to the practice most humans follow: he wrote them as himself. When confronted with the other, one has three basic options: ignore it, make it one's opposite, or make it like oneself. Malcolm X, it seems, chose the last option. He recognized that other people of color had suffered under European and American colonialism, neocolonialism, and imperialism and wanted to craft, following the Bandung conference, a global alliance of people of color. Yet, Malcolm X came to compose these suffering others as blacks rather than as "people of color." The fact of heterogeneity, it seems, was too much for Malcolm X. He drew them all together not only through the shared experience of suffering but also through the shared experience of race and thus geography—Africa.

Malcolm X did not stop at Africa writ large. He also composed the suffering of particular African locales, most prominently the Congo.[3] Like Du Bois's own move to geographic specificity in Africa, Malcolm X's is accompanied by more graphic, more detailed compositions of suffering. In "At the Audubon," delivered on December 13, 1964, Malcolm X speaks about the compositional battle that surrounds Africanist discourse in America:

> A good example of what the press can do with its images is the Congo, the area of Africa that our guest . . . is going to talk to us about tonight. Right now, in the Congo, defenseless villages are being bombed, black women and children and babies are being blown to bits by airplanes. Where do these airplanes come from? The United States, the U-n-i-t-e-d S-t-a-t-e-s. Yes, and you won't write that. You won't write that

American planes are blowing the flesh from the bodies of black women and black babies and black men. (*Malcolm X Speaks* 93)

This is far from the vague "what happens" and "touch" of Malcolm X's composition of Africa discussed above. As he moves into Africa itself, his discourse moves into the fragmented bodies of human beings. Africa leads him to the Congo, which leads him to the bits of human flesh blown apart by bombs, which leads him to the United States. Africa's allusive web of meaning finally leads him to an imagistic critique of America itself. Africa, if one takes Malcolm X's lead seriously, is not simply the land of the Nile and pyramids that schoolchildren study. Rather, Africa reveals suffering, reveals humans who are blown to bits, reveals an America that bombs the flesh off the skeletal structure of babies.

Malcolm X's composition of the Congo resonates exactly with Du Bois's. While the perpetrators in Du Bois's editorials are not Americans, they are Europeans, America's forerunners. To read Malcolm X and Du Bois on the Congo as a specific part of suffering Africa is to begin to form a particular history of the composition of this country. Where Malcolm X writes of flesh being blown off bodies, Du Bois composes the Congo in the November 1914 "World War and the Color Line" as the victim of "unspeakable atrocities" (*Selections* 1: 84). Apparently, the atrocities became speakable by June 1915. In the editorial titled "Lusitania," Du Bois foreshadows Malcolm X's specific composition, writing the natives of the Congo as a "raped and mutilated" people (*Selections* 1: 102). While it is highly doubtful that Malcolm X ever read Du Bois's editorials, they speak to Malcolm X's condition.

Africa as Monstrous/Noble

As Cone maintains, Malcolm X was well aware of the fact that Europe (and America) had negativized Africa rhetorically. Malcolm X understood part of his rhetorical task to be to challenge this negative composition of the homeland (252). Cone himself points his readers to Malcolm X's "After the Bombing" (*Malcolm X Speaks* 157–77). While other speeches are important, "After the Bombing" is an excellent point of departure.

Delivered the evening of the same day on which his house was bombed at 2:30 A.M., the speech begins with the declaration that "tonight one of the things that has to be stressed . . . is the African revolution" (158). After moving through a complex series of associative shifts, Malcolm X finally returns to this idea midway through the speech, when he begins to discuss the ways in which "they project us in the image of a criminal" (165). He claims that "they" use the press to do so and that the press, in its turn, will not challenge the "power structure" (167). "They," in this context, are the police and the government of the United States; "us" are African Americans.

After invoking images of Hitler's gas chambers in order to claim that African Americans may, one day soon, "be in one of them, just like the Jews ended up in gas ovens over there in Germany" (168), Malcolm X shifts to Africa. He begins with a series of questions:

> Now what effect does [the struggle over Africa] have on us? Why should the black man in America concern himself since he's been away from the African continent for three or four hundred years? Why should we concern ourselves? What impact does what happens to them have upon us? (168)

These questions evoke the relationship presumed to exist between European Americans and African Americans or between America and Africa—self versus other. Different here, however, is that Malcolm X applies this basic polarization to African Americans and Africans. These two groups, seemingly linked by "race," by the history of slavery, by shared oppression, are not immune to bifurcation.

In order to mend a possible split, Malcolm X declares that

> you have to realize that up until 1959 Africa was dominated by the colonial powers. Having complete control over Africa, the colonial powers of Europe projected the image of Africa negatively. They always project Africa in a negative light: jungle savages, cannibals, nothing civilized. Why then naturally it was so negative that it was negative to you and me, and you and I began to hate it. (168)

As Christopher Miller suggests, Africa is often composed as the monstrous. Malcolm X understands this to be so and attempts to objectify this negative composition in order to understand it and thereby the situation of African Americans. Malcolm X holds that "they" have used nouns to compose Africa negatively: jungle savages, cannibals. Africa, thus, is brought back as that which is other to civilized humanity.

Most pernicious for African Americans is that this negative composition affects them negatively. Malcolm X claims that this composition of Africa as savage has led African Americans to hate their own bodies: their heads, their noses, their skin color, their blood. This, in turn, has led them to hate themselves. As a result of this self-hatred, African Americans have lost confidence in themselves as productive human beings. They came to look "to the man" for help with "serious things": food, clothing, shelter, education (169).

In a few paragraphs, then, Malcolm X develops for African Americans the ramifications of the linguistic negativizing of Africa. Europe and America reached out, as Miller would say, and brought back an Africa of inferior savages. Linked to these black Africans both by skin color and the history of slavery, African Americans themselves were composed with this negative composition.

Malcolm X returned to the negative composition of Africa in a speech that followed "After the Bombing." Presented on February 16, 1965, at the Corn Hill Methodist Church in Rochester, New York, Malcolm X concentrates on the discourse surrounding events in the Congo. First, he analyzes press reports concerning the capture of Western missionaries:

> Remember how they referred to the hostages as "white hostages." Not "hostages." They said these "cannibals" in the Congo had "white hostages." Oh, and this got you all shook up. White nuns, white priests, white missionaries. What's the difference between a white hostage and a Black hostage? What's the difference between a white life and a Black life? You must think there's a difference, because your press specifies whiteness. "Nineteen white hostages" cause you to grieve in your heart. [*Laughter and applause*] (*Last Speeches* 164)

The editor's italicized note only sharpens Malcolm X's critique. It indicates that the audience, swept up in the speaker's wind, recognizes the problem of composition. Concentrating on the press's use of adjectives and nouns, Malcolm X maintains that journalists, supposedly avatars of objective informative discourse, are, in fact, biased. As they bring Africa back in writing, they bring back an Africa that is monstrously cannibalistic, the home of blacks who feast on captured white flesh. Malcolm X notes, in the paragraph that follows, that white America said nothing when "bombs were being dropped on Black people by the hundreds and the thousands." Only when a handful of missionaries, which is to say white missionaries, were captured by people of the Congo, which is to say cannibals, did Americans voice their displeasure.

Malcolm X then moves on to reflect on the composition of Africa as it affects African Americans. He first claims that "they use their ability to create images . . . to mislead people" and "to confuse the people and make the people accept wrong as right and reject right as wrong. Make the people actually think that the criminal is the victim and the victim is the criminal" (165). Thus, the negative composition of Africa is not simply the sub- or unconscious act of racists. Rather, it is a deliberate attempt to distort Africa as it really is. Africa, brought back to America in the form of discourse, became "a land of jungles, a land of animals, a land of cannibals and savages" (166). Returning to the ideas discussed in "After the Bomb," Malcolm X claims that this has led to disaster for African Americans. They have come to hate themselves and thus lose power (166–67).

However, Malcolm X does not simply analyze the negative composition of Africa. Rather, he attempts to recompose this word, to invent, as it were, new webs of meaning. In so doing, Malcolm X reveals that Africa, as a word with associative webs of meaning, is a site of inscriptive struggle. He too wants to bring Africa back to America in the form of discourse, but he wants this discourse to challenge the negative composition that dominates not only the minds of European Americans but the minds of African Americans as well.

In opposition to King, Malcolm X's composition of Africa as a site of suffering was accompanied by another dimension: he saw in Africa a noble model for the African American struggle. It is not surprising that the model he found was one that speaks of power. He brought Africa back to America in a way that emphasizes productive capabilities. Surprising is that he wrote Africa not only as a model of violent power, a place of successful and model warring revolutionaries, but also as a model economic power.

Malcolm X's composition of Africa as a model of violent power is vintage posturing. He wanted to counter King's message of nonviolence and looked to Africans who had not turned the other cheek, such as the Kenyan Mau-Mau and the Algerian revolutionaries (*Malcolm X Speaks* 8–9). His composition of Africa as a model of economic power, in contrast, is a Malcolm X rarely presented, a Malcolm X who demonstrates the ability to think in terms of economic and social growth and stability. It is one thing to change a system by bloodshed; it is another thing to move beyond the initial stages of revolution and create a society that embodies the point of the revolution.

In his December 20, 1964, speech titled "At the Audubon" (*Malcolm X Speaks* 115–36), Malcolm X composes an Africa that is a revolutionary economic powerhouse, a land that supports its own people and challenges the European and American economic order. In Egypt he finds an Aswan Dam that will create a "very fertile valley" in the desert and an industrial system that will allow Egypt to "produce their own cars, their own tractors, their own tools, their own machinery, plus a lot of other things." In Ghana, as well, Malcolm X finds the "Volta High Dam," which will allow this country to industrialize (126–27).

Malcolm X, however, does not simply stay at the specifics of Egypt and Ghana. Rather, these countries together become composed as "African nations" and then as Africa itself. He sees "African nations" that jointly become industrialized, that jointly create a "whole system" that "will be a system with a high standard but a cheaper standard of living" (127–28). This composition of the economic industrialization of African nations allows Malcolm X to write two critiques. One is of Europe and America. No longer will these countries be able to control African economies as they have in the past (128). Second, Malcolm X sees in this industrialization process a critical model for African Americans. As he says, when these countries talk

> about freedom, they're not talking about a cup of coffee with a cracker. No, they're talking about getting in a position to feed themselves and

make these other things that, when you have them, make life worth living. So this is the way you and I have to understand the world revolution that's taking place right now. (128)

The referent of the phrase "talking about a cup of coffee with a cracker" needs no elucidation, as Malcolm X well knows. Any person literate in the civil rights struggle can follow the phrase's meaning, allusive as it may appear to be to those outside this world of meaning. Yet, Malcolm X doesn't trust his audience to understand the message without his direction. The point, he claims at the end of the quotation above, is that African Americans should follow the African model, not what is being offered to them by King and others. Integration at lunch counters is one thing. Economic power is another altogether.

The late King, represented by the posthumously published piece "A Testament of Hope," would have laughed at Malcolm X. While he acknowledges that "Negroes identify understandably with Africa" (318), Africa is not, King adamantly declares, capable of offering economic aid, either in terms of real material assistance or symbolic modeling. As he claims, "American Negroes have greater economic potential than most of the nations—perhaps even more than *all* of the nations—of Africa" (319).

When King does compose Africa as noble model for African Americans, he does so most often by making Africa a member of a global list. His famous 1963 "Letter from Birmingham City Jail" offers a typical example of this strategy. Speaking of the "American Negro," King claims that

> [c]onsciously and unconsciously, he has been swept in by what the Germans call the *Zeitgeist*, and with his black brothers of Africa, and his brown and yellow brothers of Asia, South America and the Caribbean, he is moving with a sense of cosmic urgency toward the promised land of racial justice. (297)

With allusions to German philosophy and to the Bible, themselves part of our cultural archives, King composes Africa as a site of solidarity in the context of the noble global struggle of people of color. The sense of nobility is heightened by King's reference to divine inspiration and end. These people of color are informed by the cosmos, and they seek "the promised land." Black, brown, yellow: all people are part of what King calls the "inescapable network of mutuality" ("A Christmas Sermon on Peace" 254). Yet, there is nothing particularly distinct about Africa, here.

King does claim in the "*Playboy* Interview" that "[w]e are descendants of the Africans. Our heritage is Africa. We should never seek to break the ties, nor should the Africans" (364). Yet even this claim follows what is, almost word for word, the same remark he makes in the letter quoted above. The interviewer then asked King to speak about Africa, specifically. King did so, but with a caveat. Africa, finally, should work to remind the United States not that Negro Americans are the special property of Africa, but that the struggle of African Americans "is part of a worldwide struggle." It is not limited to Africa or America. It is, as King emphasizes throughout his discourse, part of global struggle of people of color.

While it is fair to assume that King's composition of Africa's noble stature as a part of the global struggle of people of color responds to the negativizing of Africa, King himself never discusses the negative. Unlike Malcolm X, who was keenly aware of the negative, King accentuates only the positive. He leaves the negative untreated. So too Du Bois leaves the negative unspoken.

Unlike Malcolm X, Du Bois did not compose Africa either as a model of violent revolution or as a model of economic power and independence. Unlike King, Du Bois did compose Africa as offering something unique to African Americans. The compositions of Africa he brings to his audiences in the pages of the *Crisis* are a site of pan-African possibility and, most importantly for this essay, the land of Ethiopia.

Du Bois's pan-African work has been dealt with in detail by many other scholars and critics, so I need not rehearse it here. Suffice it to say that Du Bois attempted to compose Africa as a micro–United Nations that would address that problems of the continent, challenge European and American world domination, and speak for Negroes everywhere.

More fascinating than his pan-African compositions of Africa is his turn, or even return, to Ethiopia as a metaphor for Africa, as a vision for African Americans. As Christopher Miller informs his readers, Ethiopia has longed served as an object of Africanist discourse, dating at least to Homer (24). While it has been composed both positively and negatively, "the prospect of delight" that Homer composes "is one that the ancient view of Ethiopia seems to hold today" (24). Du Bois is no different, and his play, his pageant, or rather, his enormous piece of performance art, "The Star of Ethiopia," composes Ethiopia, and thus Africa, as a "*holy thing*" ("The Drama Among Black Folk," *Selections* 1: 121).

To remain focused on Du Bois's work in the *Crisis*, the text of "The Star of Ethiopia" is not the concern here. Rather, the concern is the ways in which Du Bois uses his pageant in the *Crisis* to compose Africa. This composition first begins with Du Bois's inclusion of text from the pageant in the *Crisis*. Opening the editorial titled "The Drama Among Black Folk" is the claim that Ethiopia is the "*Eldest and Strongest of the Races of men whose faces be Black*" (121). Early into the editorial Du Bois refines this with yet another piece from the pageant: here he claims that Ethiopia is the "*All-mother of men*" (121). Du Bois's point is clear early on in this editorial. Ethiopia represents not only Africa but all of humanity; it is the best of the black races. It is the womb and nurturer of human life itself. Thus, Du Bois implies, African Americans can look to Africa with not simply a sense of pride for their ancestral homeland but with a sense of awful wonder: as Negroes, they stand in direct connection to the mother of humanity.[4]

The rest of the editorial, one of his most complex, is at once a collage of Du Bois's language and those of reviewers and the pageant itself. In the middle of the editorial is a fascinating line of Du Bois's own words, powerfully challenged by the text of the pageant. Du Bois claims that he wanted to teach "the colored people themselves the meaning of their history and their rich, emotional life" and "to reveal the Negro to the white world as a human, feeling thing" (122). Yet, as was discussed above, the text of the pageant itself offers a much grander and a much more radical vision. The history he offers to "the colored people themselves" is the history of the mother of humanity. The Negro he reveals to the white world is more than "a human, feeling thing." The Negro, the pageant claims, is heir to Ethiopia, thus heir to the status of all-mother.

A later editorial, written in response to World War I, only supports this reading of the contradictory nature of Du Bois's composition of his pageant. He claims that Negroes, fighting in the war, are "the Ancient of Days, the First of Races, and the Oldest of Men. Before Time was, we are" ("A Philosophy in Time of War," *Selections* 1: 160). This composition moves Negroes to a superior or even an originary position that is beyond and before the white world that oppresses them. It also composes Africa as the Ur-home, as the extraordinary space that African Americans can claim in the face of a hostile white world. This composition of Africa hints at Du Bois's Edenic desires, which are, together with those of King and Malcolm X, the subject of the next chapter. Eden, for all three, is the telos of emancipatory composition.

5 | Eden

> Art's utopia, the counterfactual yet-to-come, is draped
> in black. It goes on being a recollection of the possible
> with a critical edge against the real; it is a kind of
> imaginary restitution of that catastrophe, which is world
> history.
>
> —Theodor W. Adorno, *Aesthetic Theory*

As Thomas Merton, the Trappist monk and social critic, argues, "Eden" has historical importance for America. Europeans came to this continent, in part, with the feeling of "an Adam newly restored to paradise" (109).[1] Thus, the origins of the republic now called the United States are intimately tied to a vision of Eden, to a search, as the conquistadores would have it in their version, for Eldorado.

Not surprisingly, given the religious impulses that mark the history of its colonization and given its rootedness in biblical narrative, drama, and poetry, American culture is deeply informed by Eden. Yet, the allusive play of Eden is not limited to the life of religious institutions, be they Christian or Jewish. It is certainly true that members of these local cultures—part of the American culture at large— need to know Eden. Within Christianity, for instance, there is a tradition of metaphoric play that names Jesus as the "second Adam."

Nor is the allusive play of Eden limited to the life of academic institutions, in particular the academy that preserves and teaches the canon of literary texts, most notably Milton's *Paradise Lost.* Certainly, one must be able to play allusively with Eden if one is to delve fully into Milton's exploration. While crucial to Western culture in general and American culture in particular, such texts are read, in the main, by the members of a professional class and their students. It is a fair assumption that the vast majority of Americans never encounter Eden through Milton or any of the other texts of the literary canon. They do, however, encounter Eden in the popular, public discourse of the republic.

Consider, for instance, *InStyle* magazine. A child of the better-known *People* magazine, *InStyle* particularly focuses on what the "television personality" Robin Leach called "the lifestyles of the rich and famous." The August 1995 issue contains a story by David Hutchins, titled "A Little Piece of Heaven," which chronicles the rural Montana dream home of actress Andie McDowell and her husband, "ex-model" Paul Qualley.[2] The title of the piece reveals immediately the allusive play in which the article is engaged. The memory of Eden is invoked; heaven and earth are merged on earth in a specific locale. Eden, as this article plays with it, shifts to a distinctly American space, away from where it is often presumed to be located—at the confluence of the Tigris and Euphrates Rivers in Mesopotamia.

The title, however, is not all. The lead to the story that appears with the table of contents refers even more specifically to Eden. It tells the issue's readers that McDowell and Qualley, "on 3,000 glorious acres in Montana . . . create an earthly paradise for themselves and their children" (5). Simply put, readers of this article will not be able to feel its complex texture unless they are able to make the allusive connections to Eden.

So too *Legends of the Fall* composes a vision of Eden—in Montana not incidentally—but with a native twist. Disgusted by the American treatment of the native peoples of the country, the colonel, in a dramatic moment, drives his officer's sword into the ground and resigns his commission. He then establishes a beautiful Montana ranch where European Americans and indigenous peoples live and work together, enjoying the fruits of a bounteous nature. The colonel's friend—a Cheyenne—helps raise the colonel's three boys, teaching them the mysteries of the land. So too the ranch shelters and supports a miscegenous couple: one of the hands is married to a Native woman with whom he has had a daughter.

After an extended exploration of the Fall, the colonel's middle son, Tristan, returns to Eden. He comes home to the ranch to find natural harmony and interracial love. He helps the ranch restore itself and marries, significantly, the "half-breed" daughter of the ranch hand and his wife. While Eden is eventually lost again, the film offers a lyrical interlude of paradise: Tristan and his wife literally become the new Adam and Eve, frolicking with horses, with the land, with each other, all the while fruitfully producing children.

Viewers of this film will not be able to feel its complex texture unless they are able to make the allusive connections to Eden that fill it. Certainly, one of the legends of the Fall, the state in which we all live, is the legend of Eden. We have heard of it but have not known it ourselves. The movie *Legends of the Fall* invokes the garden, placing it in America as a way to speak to the American condition.

It might be tempting at this point to invoke Kenneth Burke's discussions of Eden in order to consider further the place of Eden in the American republic. As perhaps the preeminent American rhetorical theorist, Burke treats Eden in order to discuss the logological nature of reality. It is certainly true that Eden is a linguistic construction, a metaphor for the ways in which humans seek a unitary term, a unified state of linguistic rest.

However, Eden is more than a metaphor for the desire of language. It also marks the desire for place. As Ernst Bloch writes regarding the myth of St. Brendan, humans long "for the golden somewhere of an enclave of happiness which escaped the Fall" (2: 763). Bloch discusses many types of utopic longing—technological and architectural among them—but concludes that Eden (and its correspondent metaphor, Eldorado) "comprehensively embraces the other . . . utopias." Eden, thus, is the Ur-utopia, the utopia of utopias (2: 793–94).

While *InStyle* and *Legends of the Fall* both compose Eden within America, they differ significantly about the inhabitants of the garden. *InStyle* reflects the white dream: Eden comprises white Adam and Eve and their children. *Legends of the Fall*, in contrast, complicates this order, envisioning a reversal of white domination, imagining an interracial Eden. But even *Legends of the Fall* does not deal with the problem of African Americans. It focuses, rather, on the originary peoples of North America, inscribing an Eden where the children of Europe and the children of the tribes live harmoniously with the land and each other. The children of Africa are nowhere to be seen.

It is within this context that the Edenic work of Du Bois, King, and Malcolm X should be placed. Each draws on this word that is central to America, yet they find within Eden the "other side." They compose an Eden that fundamentally challenges the republic itself.

As is the case with the Fall, Eden works implicitly in their texts. Nonetheless, one cannot grasp their rhetorics fully without playing in the word's allusive world. Consider, for instance, an Edenic fragment of King's "I Have a Dream" speech:

> I have a dream that one day every valley shall be exalted, every hill and mountain shall be made low, the rough places shall be made plain [sic], and the crooked places shall be made straight and the glory of the Lord will be revealed and all flesh shall see it together. (219)

King's dream is a vision of paradise, as will be discussed more fully below. It is a dream of a geographical utopia wherein humans experience God directly. It is a vision of a world beyond the push and pull, the give and take, of democracy.

Given this vision, the U.S. celebration of King's birthday as a national holiday is decidedly ironic. The King that we celebrate is a King who envisions a space, a place, beyond mere civil rights. King sees beyond a society forever caught in the competing oppositions composed by John Locke and Thomas Jefferson, oppositions checked by the balance of power. King is not merely a Ciceronian democrat; he is a dreamer of Eden.

This is true of Malcolm X and Du Bois, as well. Read with Eden in mind, the works of these three suggest a possibility of human existence beyond democratic order. They see paradise, thus confirming, conserving, the place of Eden in American culture. Yet, they move beyond America, beyond the European American dreams of Eden in the new country. Each, with Eden in sight, finds America wanting. Thus, they are models of emancipatory composition, radicals in the full sense of the word.

Malcolm X

It may be the case that Malcolm X, as Cone argues, predominantly experienced America as a nightmare. To indulge, for a moment, in biographical criticism, Malcolm X's life may have made it impossible for him to see, beyond a dim glimmer, the Edenic possibilities envisioned by both Du Bois and King.

Undeniably, King and Du Bois, as African Americans, suffered the effects of the color line. Yet, they also profited from the beneficence of bourgeois culture. Considering the fact that they were African Americans born into a white-dominated society, both had relatively comfortable childhoods. Du Bois remembers his own place of birth and rearing as a paradise in and of itself. King, likewise, was raised under the protection of Daddy King and the black church. So too both Du Bois and King graduated from high school, attended excellent undergraduate institutions, earned Ph.D.'s, and worked for decent wages under the protection of religious and secular institutions. If any two African American leaders were predisposed to find the Edenic possibilities within America, they were Du Bois and King.

Malcolm X, as is well known, suffered terribly under the pressure of the color line. His grandmother was raped by a European American, thus giving him a fair skin tone and the hair for which he became known as "Detroit Red." His father, a Garveyite lay minister, was probably murdered by a white racist mob. Malcolm X dropped out of high school because a teacher was incapable of helping him envision a life beyond the rigid stereotypes of the color line. As a train porter, a shoe-shine worker, a hustler, Malcolm X suffered under European American oppression and saw European American depravity (sexual and otherwise) in ways that Du Bois and King did not. It is not surprising, at least biographically, that Malcolm X predominantly composed a nightmare and only tentatively, hesitantly, composed Edenic desires.

When he did, these desires were linked to Africa. Much has already been made of Malcolm X's composition of Africa as a homeland. As George Breitman, editor of *Malcolm X Speaks*, suggests, Malcolm X advocated Africa, for much of his career, as the place to which African Americans should return as soon as possible (*Malcolm X Speaks*

18–20). Even though Malcolm X began to back away from this dream after his separation from the Nation of Islam, it still offers a glimpse into his Edenic desires.

While Malcolm X never fully explores what a separatist return to Africa might actually entail, he hints at its Edenic nature in one of the final speeches he delivered as a member of the Nation of Islam, "God's Judgment of White America (The Chickens Are Coming Home to Roost)" (*End* 121–48). With a call to "America" to "atone for her crimes" against African Americans, Malcolm X suggests "that the race problem can easily be solved, just by sending these twenty-two million ex-slaves *back to our own homeland* where we can live in peace and harmony with our own kind" (147). As sketchy as this proposal is, it contains one important feature: the return would allow African Americans to live in peace and harmony. With the move, African Americans would be able to leave behind the divisiveness of the Fall.

Malcolm X also suggests that if America is unwilling to let African Americans return to Africa, then it should set aside land within the Western Hemisphere for a separatist garden. This is not to be taken seriously, however, because he leaves this idea as quickly as he comes to it, returning again to the homeland theme. His suggestion of a separatist state within the hemisphere can be understood, rather, as a ruse: if you don't give us Africa, then give us a piece of your land instead.

In the previous paragraph, I use the phrase "separatist garden" deliberately. Malcolm X did not simply envision political peace and harmony. Echoing his claims that real revolution is about land rather than integrated cups of coffee, Malcolm X does not simply demand a return to Africa. He also demands "fertile, productive land on which we can farm and provide our own people with sufficient food, clothing, and shelter" (148). By the end of his career as a minister of the Nation of Islam, Malcolm X envisions a state in which African Americans can live in peace and harmony, where they can work the land to fulfill their needs.

This vision of land, in particular African land, intensifies in later letters and speeches, after Malcolm X broke with the Nation of Islam. While it is true, as Breitman and Cone hold, that Malcolm X came more fully to anchor himself in the American Civil Rights movement, he still longed for Africa and the garden it promised. In a May 1964 letter from Ghana, for instance, he writes of the "great fertility" and extraordinary vegetation of Africa. Though the letter ends with a commitment to the American civil rights struggle, it also ends with a commitment to the pan-African movement. Malcolm wants to live in America but looks always to Africa (*Malcolm X Speaks* 62–63).

By his December 20, 1964, speech, "At the Audubon," Malcolm X had intensified this vision of the fertility of Africa (*Malcolm X Speaks* 105–36). Arguing that Africa is caught in the geopolitical, Cold War struggle between East and West, he claims that "they want you and me to think Africa is jungle, of no value, of no consequence" (122). However, Malcolm X offers a different angle. First, and less important for this chapter, Africa is of great political consequence. It is, most importantly, the home of the Suez Canal.

Africa is also the Edenic garden undiscovered. Malcolm X writes that

[i]t's so heavily vegetated that you can take any section of Africa and use modern agricultural methods and turn that section alone into the breadbasket for the world. . . . It's rich. A jungle is only a place that's heavily vegetated—the soil is so rich and the climate is so good that everything grows, and it doesn't grow in season—it grows all the time. All the time is the season. That means it can grow anything, produce anything. (122)

His geographical hyperbole only intensifies Malcolm X's Edenic composition of Africa. Certainly, the Sahara is not fertile. Yet, Malcolm X here envisions the entire continent as a brimming, fecund garden, a place that is more fertile, potentially more productive than any other place on earth.

This emphasis on productivity, however, is what dulls the Edenic sheen. Malcolm X composes Africa as the garden only to turn immediately and think of it in geopolitical terms. The garden does not exist as a place beyond the vicissitudes of human history. Rather, Malcolm X wants to turn the garden into a place from which Africans can assert global political power. Thus, Eden is not simply an end; it is, in addition, a place of refuge, retreat, and strength from which African Americans can affect the world.

Du Bois

Du Bois is the master of the American Eden. If at the end of his life he had rejected America for exile in Ghana, his early career at the *Crisis* was deeply American. While he sarcastically, ironically, hyperbolically criticized a country that had failed its own founding intentions, he also used elements of the American experience to write Eden, to compose his paradisiacal desires.

Du Bois's use of America to compose his Edenic longing is manifest as early as the January 1911 *Crisis* (*Selections* 1: 1–2). In an editorial titled "A Winter Pilgrimage," Du Bois reports of his travels "to different groups of colored people in this land" (1). The title of the editorial indicates the nature of the piece: Du Bois is traveling to holy ground.

Oberlin College, a place long dedicated to emancipation, to social justice, is such ground. Set off in its own paragraph is Du Bois's introduction to Oberlin, an alternative to what he found in Toledo and Cleveland: "Between these cities of past and present lies the mystic city of the future, with its great cloud walls" (1). Oberlin provides an alternative vision to a troubled world. It is the earthly, American embodiment of paradisiacal longing. Even more important than the expository declaration that Oberlin is the "mystic city of the future" is the description that ends the sentence: it has "great cloud walls." The clouds connote numerous dimensions of the city. It is hidden. It is mysterious. It is protected not by bricks and mortar but by vapor.

Behind these clouds is a model school and city. European American and African American students "walk on sacred ground" where "the spirit of democracy is strong, the influence of the faculty is righteous" (1). Although Du Bois admits that some problems of "the Present" intrude—much as the serpent was present in the garden—he finds Oberlin to be the kind of place where the daughter of a "brown father, a yellow mother" entertains with her parents in their parlor "the white pastor and the white girl chum" (2). Oberlin is the mystical, shrouded city of harmony against which "the bonds of medievalism are drawn" (2).

At Oberlin, Du Bois finds a human polity, a city organized in a way nearly unimaginable, a culture that embodies what is hidden in the future behind clouds. By 1913 Du Bois began to weave nature itself into his paradisiacal visions of human polity. This moved him toward the Edenic revelations of Africa, which he discovered later. In his autobiography, Du Bois writes that

> I was born by a golden river and in the shadow of two great hills, five years after the Emancipation Proclamation, which began the freeing of American Negro slaves. The valley was wreathed in grass and trees and crowned to the eastward by the huge bulk of East Mountain, with crag and cave and dark forests. Westward the hill was gentler, rolling up to gorgeous sunsets and cloud-swept storms . . . the climate was to our thought quite perfect. (*Autobiography* 61)

Of crucial import in this autobiographical reflection is that Du Bois brings together culture and nature in a moment of desire fulfilled. His entrance into a "valley wreathed in grass and trees" came at a time when America had begun its attempt to fulfill itself. The slaves had been freed; the war was over; the Union had been saved. Du Bois does not remember idyllic nature apart from culture. Rather, the two are melded, inseparable, interpenetrating each other.[3]

Nature in this autobiographical scene is nothing less than an American Eden. The climate is "perfect." The valley is at once royal (crowned by a mysterious mountain) and revelatory of sublime beauty (to the west "gorgeous sunsets and cloud-swept storms"). As an old man, Du Bois finds in his childhood a moment of paradise marked historically by a human culture that had, finally, outlawed slavery.

Du Bois, in the pages of the *Crisis*, returns to his childhood, finding in America places where human and natural polity reflected Eden. One such place was Seattle. By July 1913, Du Bois had discovered in the American northwest a place unlike any other, including his beloved Oberlin.

In the editorial titled "I Go A-Talking," Du Bois again reports on his travels across America (*Selections* 1: 58–61). While many places—including Indianapolis, St. Louis, Kansas City, Los Angeles, and San Francisco—offered promise, Du Bois found in Seattle something special. He writes that "the wonderful Western pilgrimage was crowned at Seattle. The magic city of 300,000 lies on its hills above silvery waters, dream-beautiful" (60). The word pilgrimage again comes into play here, as it did in Du Bois's editorial about Oberlin. Clearly, Du Bois understood his travels around the country as journeys in search of holy spaces.

Too, Du Bois found in Seattle a "group of men" who "were unusual in vigor and individuality," a group whose equal Du Bois had seldom seen (60). In all, then, Du Bois found in Seattle a melding of the natural and human, a city that resonates with the memory of his childhood spent in a place marked by both the sublime beauty of the natural order and the Emancipation Proclamation, a place that resonates with dreams of paradise—vigorous people living in a magic city that is "dream-beautiful" "above silvery waters."

Moreover—and this is perhaps the most significant part of the editorial—Du Bois tells his readers that his trip to the northwest, crowned by his visit to Seattle, led to a moment of communion with God:

> For one day I turned my back on the perfect memory of this golden journey and sailed out across the seas and thanked God for this the kindliest race on His green earth, for whom I had the privilege of working and to whom I had the pride of belonging. (60)

Here it is not clear what Du Bois means, exactly, by the phrase "sailed out across the seas."[4] The import, however, is clear. The northwest in general, and Seattle in particular, provided Du Bois with a moment away from the struggle against the color line. They provided him the opportunity to encounter God, the opportunity to link together God, the "green earth," and people of African descent.

As if he could not shake his trip west out of his mind, Du Bois returned to it in a September 1913 article titled, appropriately and pointedly, "The Great Northwest" (*Selections* 1: 67–68). It begins with a lyrical reflection on the natural beauty, the "tall black mountains and ghostlike trees, snow and the echo of ice on the hills." This reflection on nature, however, quickly turns into a reflection on time and space. Du Bois finds, under the "creeping spell of the silent ocean with its strange metamorphoses of climate, its seasons of rain and shine," that one's calendar becomes confused, that one loses one's sense of bearing (67). The "Great Northwest" removes humans from ordered time and space. It seems, at least for this moment, a place of grand beauty and mystery beyond human history.

It is also a place where Du Bois finds people who are "one with the land" and who seek others to join them in order to "find freedom," to live in a climate that is "mild and alluring," to live in a geography of "mountains and sea." Du Bois resoundingly ends this piece with "Come!"

The magic of this place leads Du Bois, on his way out of "fairyland back to the world again," to imagine a new space, even beyond Seattle, a space that combines the best of the American West with a sprinkle of Europe:

> [S]ome city set like Seattle on a hill with the roses of Los Angeles and the Golden Gate of San Francisco in the dim distance and the Grand Canyon looming down from heaven. Through that city two great and thick-thronged avenues cross forming four arms—Prince's Street in Edinburgh is one, the Elysian Fields of Paris another, Orange Grove Avenue of Pasadena is a third, and the fourth may be the Kansas City Paseo, or Piccadilly—I am not sure which. Then high in that central square I think would be fit place for the Throne of God. (68)

This vision, whose impulse was the northwest in general and Seattle in particular, reveals Du Bois's longing for a place that Edenically weaves together the human and natural orders and, in so doing, brings God again into the direct presence of humankind. In this vision, the natural actually takes precedence. The human order is relatively unspecific, marked only by city and avenue names. The cities, finally, are included only for their physical attributes. For instance, Los Angeles is invoked for its roses; San Francisco for its gate and thus the ocean, bay, and mountains for which it provides relief. Most remarkable about Seattle is its natural environment. For extraordinary grandeur, Du Bois includes the Grand Canyon "looming down from heaven," thus connecting this earthly place with the heavenly.

Du Bois dreams, finally, of an Edenic city that is far away from the Ciceronian republic that is America at its best. If the end of the republic for most of us is a country wherein democracy flourishes, the end of the republic for Du Bois, at least the Du Bois of 1913, is a place well beyond the push and pull of democracy.

By August 1921, Du Bois had come to refine his Edenic vision even further, at this point rejecting even the metaphor of city and nature woven together. If in Oberlin he found an Edenic city without the natural, and if in the northwest he found the impulse for a vision of an Edenic city wherein the natural and the human integrated so perfectly as to invite the presence of God, by 1921 Du Bois moved to nature without city, foreshadowing the Edenic revelations of Africa.

In the August 1921 piece titled "Hopkinsville, Chicago and Idlewild," Du Bois finds in Idlewild—a resort community for African Americans—Eden (*Selections* 1: 305–7). As he says at the end of the piece, Idlewild offers "drinking water straight from the hills of Paradise" (307). Much of the piece is lyrical reflection on the beauty of Idlewild.

> I have seen the moon rising above purple waters against the velvet background of tall and silent trees.
>
> I have seen the mystery of Dawn, the filmy mists that swathed the light limbs of the world, the hush of dreamless sleep, the chill of conquered death and then—the wide, wild thunder of the rising sun. (306)

The import of these lines hardly needs elucidation. Du Bois here composes the American Eden, the garden undisturbed. Yet, it is not simply a natural scene. While Du Bois has given up on the metaphor of the city present in his earlier visions, he does include human culture. At Idlewild he meets other folks—African Americans all—who have traveled from the "earth's ends," who have worked "within the Veil," who have, in a line that reminds one of Malcolm X, triumphed "over the White Devils of America" (306). Du Bois delights in their company and calls on other African Americans to join them in this African American Eden, which can become, Du Bois thinks, "a center of Negro art, conference and recreation" (307). This Eden is not a place of hiding. It is a place of retreat set against the greater world that is captive to the color line.

In a significant line at the beginning of this lyrical exploration, Du Bois remarks that all the people he has met are "sons and great-grandchildren of Ethiopia" (306). This is not simply an Edenic haven for African Americans who need respite from the battle against the color line; it is the gathering place, in America, of an Ethiopian remnant. Coming home to Eden is a group of people who are not just people. They are, in Du Bois's vision, the originary people, children of the mother who gave to all humankind iron, faith, humility, pain, and, most importantly, eternal freedom.

Du Bois's vision of this African American Eden could not be more different from most of our dreams of America. While the King holiday celebrates a vision of an integrated wonderland, Du Bois, King's forebear, had by 1921 played within Eden's allusive web in order to invoke a separatist space that provided retreat to the children of the all-mother. This space allows African Americans the opportunity to come together in solidarity against the "White Devils" who rule the country.

As Merton suggests, it is traditional for European Americans to cast Eden as America, America as Eden. Thus, Du Bois's composition of Eden by way of the American landscape is fundamentally radical in a fully American sense. While envisioning a place beyond the vicissitudes of democracy, beyond even our wildest dreams of a fully functioning Ciceronian republic, Du Bois roots this place in America itself. The end is extreme but familiar. While he composes the children of Ethiopia settled into an African American Eden, the Eden is, still, American.

However, Du Bois takes this word, Eden, and moves it beyond America into one of America's primary others—Africa. The land from which early Americans, even the Founding Fathers, gathered their human chattel is used by Du Bois as a way to compose his Edenic longing, longing that cannot be met, apparently, by the American republic itself. American Ciceronian democracy, as integrated as it may be, is inadequate. So too, however, is an American Eden. Du Bois longs for an Edenic space outside out of America.

Du Bois, in contrast to King, finds in Africa an Edenic possibility. In contrast to Malcolm X, Du Bois composes Africa Edenically not in order to assert the possibility of global, geopolitical power but rather to dream of a place of rest, of harmony, of peace beyond the color line.

In a series of three *Crisis* pieces—"Sketches from Abroad: *Le Grand Voyage*" (*Selections* 1: 381–84), "Africa" (385–90), and "Little Portraits of Africa" (391–93), Du Bois writes of his journey to "the Eternal World of Black Folk" (381). At the beginning of "Sketches," Du Bois remarks that he has seen "all the states of the American *Empire*" (emphasis mine) and much of Europe. While kindly and interesting, these areas of the world are, as Du Bois notes, "painfully white" (381). Looking forward to Africa, Du Bois, by the end of "Sketches," writes of Spain. He notes that "always and everywhere there is going on a subtle change. My brown face attracts no attention. I am darker than my neighbors but they are dark. I become, quite to my own surprise, simply a man" (383). Thus, as he moves south toward Africa, Du Bois finds himself in a way he never can in the white world. In Lisbon, he tells his readers, he shared conversation (in French, of course, echoing his demand that French become the *lingua franca* of the African diaspora) and cigarettes with a Spaniard who was polite, even brotherly. Du Bois contrasts this man with a New Yorker who would, Du Bois assures his readers, "have shouldered me warily and explained on the other side the ubiquity of 'damn niggers!' " (384).

The essay titled "Africa" is remarkable for its heady euphoria marking Du Bois's initial foray into "The Eternal World of Black Folk." It begins even before Du Bois enters the land, shipboard on December 20. At sunset, he finds "the sun, a dull gold ball, strange shaped and rayless" and a sky that shifted from "violet blue and grey" to "blue-green" (386). Du Bois here demonstrates again his fine eye for natural phenomenon. He was not, simply, a political man concerned only about human culture. Rather, as should be evident by now, Du Bois, the dapper New Yorker, was deeply informed by the landscape of his birth and childhood. For Du Bois, nature and human culture belong together; Du Bois's Eden comprised both.

While "Africa" speaks mainly of Du Bois's time in Liberia, "resting under the shock of war," thus admitting the presence of non-Edenic life, it nonetheless composes Eden, marking the paradisiacal gathering of nature and human culture. Du Bois writes, for instance, of a Christmas dinner he shared with a family (388). While the Christ child is noticeably absent, the Edenic gathering of nature and human is not. The eldest daughters "wore, on the beautiful black skin of their necks, the exquisite gold chains of the Liberian artisan." The youngest daughter's hair, "dark" with "thick curls," was festooned with a "wide pink ribbon," a ribbon "that lay like sudden sunlight on the shadows." The playing of children and the dinner—abundant with "duck, chicken, beef, rice, plantain and collards, cake, tea, water, and Madeira wine"—was crowned by the grace of nature. Du Bois writes that "we went and looked at the heavens, the uptwisted sky—Orion and Cassiopeia at zenith; the Little Bear beneath the horizon, new unfamiliar sights in the Milky Way—all awry, a-living—sun for snow at Christmas, and happiness and cheer" (388).

At one level, the natural landscape—as it is represented by the stars—is odd to Du Bois: he is accustomed to the North American skies. Yet, despite its oddness, it stands as a crown to the human interaction of the feast. It is Christmas Day, and Du Bois is full of "happiness and cheer." He is with Africans, he eats abundantly, and he finds in the heavens brilliantly shining constellations—familiar and unfamiliar—gracing the scene.

This initial foray into the African Eden finds its culmination in "Little Portaits of Africa." This piece begins with a foreshadowing of Malcolm X's own Edenic desires: "Africa is vegetation. It is the riotous, unbridled bursting life of leaf and limb" (391). Du Bois finds in Africa the organic fecundity of the garden itself. His Massachusetts valley was naturally rich, but Africa is richness par excellence. While much of the piece contains more lyrical reflections on the amazing Edenic splendor of the place—both natural and human—most important, finally, is the end. Here one reads Du Bois's Edenic desires fully manifest in the pages of the *Crisis*. Here one reads his rejection of the American Eden for that in, that of, Africa.

Rapturously, Du Bois claims that Africa "is a world—a universe of itself and for itself" and, as such, is truly home: this is where "the Spirit longs to die" (392). With honesty, Du Bois does not claim that Africa is Eden. Rather, it contains the Edenic potential he explored in numerous places in America, only to reject them all. He holds that with work

> there will spring in Africa a civilization without coal, without noise, where machinery will sing and never rush and roar, and where men will sleep and think and dance and lie prone before the rising sons, and women will be happy.
>
> The objects of life will be revolutionized. Our duty will not consist in getting up at seven, working furiously for six, ten and twelve hours,

eating in sullen ravenousness or extraordinary repletion. No—We shall dream the day away and in cool dawns, in little swift hours, do all our work. (393)

The Edenic quality of this vision needs little elucidation, but I want to make two points. Du Bois, importantly, is not a neo-Luddite. Technology has a place, but it is technology far beyond that of the polluted world in which Du Bois lived. It is a technology that serves the harmonious relationship between the people and the land. Also, Du Bois's Edenic vision is rooted in the African landscape. As an American attempting to subvert the color line, Du Bois leaves America in order to offer a composition of paradise. To follow him, to have students follow him, is to leave America itself.

King

King never cast a Du Boisian gaze upon Africa. Even at the end of his career, when he was most disenchanted with America, most skeptical at the prospects of the American republic fulfilling its destiny, King did not turn to Africa as a way out, did not seek to make the African other his own.

Rather, Africa always remained for King a site of suffering, a site deeply marked by the Fall. At least twice, early in his public career, he reminds his audience that Africa is the originary geographical point of American slavery. King thus uses Africa as part of a negative analogic scheme that opens Africa's other—America—to profound criticism. Africa never serves as an Edenic other used to criticize America. Rather, it is Africa fallen, Africa as the origin of slaves. Consider this sequence of lines from King's 1957 "Nonviolence and Racial Injustice":

> The first Negroes landed on the shores of this nation in 1619, one year ahead of the Pilgrim Fathers. They were brought here from Africa and, unlike the Pilgrims, they were brought here against their will, as slaves. Throughout the era of slavery the Negro was treated in inhuman fashion. He was considered a thing to be used, not a person to be respected. (5)

King suggests here that the slaves are to Africa and America exactly *not* what the Pilgrims are to Europe and America. The slaves were brought from Africa. They did not bring themselves, searching for refuge from tyranny, searching for Eden. The Pilgrims, in contrast, brought themselves from Europe, a religious people on pilgrimage. For the slaves, Africa stands not as home rejected but as home denied. America stands not as home, but as prison. King nonetheless never looked back to Africa as the promised land, as Eden. King's dream seems to rest in America, at least at first glance.

This "dream" has been the subject of intense and lengthy discussion among students of King.[5] While much insight can be gleaned from a study of this conversation, only Keith Miller has begun to articulate the extraordinary radicality of King's vision (146–48). Allusively playing with the Bible and American cultural documents, King, as Miller eloquently states,

> projected the end of history, when brotherhood will triumph, identities will converge, and sacred time will reign. Justice will pour down like waters, valleys will become mountains, and the stone hewn from the mountain will smash all racist, earthly kingdoms. (148)

Finally, King did not envision a fully functioning Ciceronian democracy. Rather, King looked beyond democracy to a time when history itself has ended, to a time of Edenic desire made manifest on Earth.

Consider King's famous "I Have a Dream" speech, delivered at the March on Washington. The speech, as Miller holds, "envisions a day when everyone will dismantle social barriers and merge voices by singing 'America' " (147). That "I Have a Dream" composes Eden is made manifestly clear in the fifth dream:

> I have a dream that one day every valley shall be exalted, every hill and mountain shall be made low, the rough places shall be made plain, and the crooked places shall be made straight and the glory of the Lord will be revealed and all flesh shall see it together. (King 219)

This culminating vision makes sacred both landscape and human polity. Brought together here are not only the "sons of former slaves and slave owners" but also sons of former slaves and slave owners from the "red hills of Georgia." Transformed here are not only the people of Mississippi but also the state itself: it will become "an oasis of freedom and justice," a *place* in which all Americans find each other as siblings. Importantly, the ultimate moment of the dream is a moment of revelation, of divine-human relationship. As in the garden, "all flesh shall see" God in God's glory. The separation of human and divine that marks the biblical narrative of the Fall will be overcome in this vision.

Yet, while "it is a dream deeply rooted in the American dream," it is only *rooted* (219). That is to say, King acknowledges his source in the American founding documents, but his vision finally goes beyond the dream of egalitarian democracy into the utopia of Eden, where valleys are "exalted," where humans again behold "the glory of the Lord."

As Cone argues, this speech was the high point in King's Americanism. The King adored—and I choose this verb with the utmost purposefulness, intending it to be read for all its religious import—by America is the "I Have a Dream" King. America sees this King as one who still composes America as a country that can fulfill its latent desires of egalitarian democracy.

This vision of King is doubly problematic. First, as Keith Miller argues, King does not envision an egalitarian democracy, despite the fact that he works with the classical American rhetorical tradition. King envisions a utopia—Eden—that goes beyond American democracy. King's vision is not one where humans can rationally discuss the problems of the day, working together toward equitable solutions. Rather, King sees a profound communion of landscape and human polity and God.

Second, the American iconization of the "I Have a Dream" King is problematic because it freezes King at a time convenient to American longing. It refuses to see the internationalist King, the King who, as Cone teaches, soundly, devastatingly criticizes America. It hides the King of Christmas Eve 1967, the King who revisits his former self. In "A Christmas Sermon on Peace," King refines his dream, recognizing that is was too myopic, too limited (253–58).

The sermon begins with a somber note: "The Christmas season finds us a rather bewildered human race. . . . Our world is sick with war; everywhere we turn we see its ominous possibilities" (253). However, ever the good preacher, King quickly offers a dialectical turn. Though the world suffers sickness, there is hope—the utopian possibilities inherent in the Christmas season.

As an antidote to the sickness, King tells his audience that they must dedicate themselves anew to "nonviolence, its philosophy and its strategy." Moreover, they are not to limit themselves to the American scene: "[I]f we are to have peace on earth, our loyalties must become ecumenical rather than sectional. Our loyalties must transcend our race, our tribe, our class, and our nation; and this means we must develop a world perspective" (253). This, then, is the King who composes the Orient and, to a lesser extent, Africa. This is not the "I Have a Dream" King, adored as a trumpeter of the latent egalitarian possibilities of American culture; rather, it is a King looking outward to a world that is "caught in an inescapable network of mutuality" (254).

It is also the King who, later in the sermon, decries the "I Have a Dream" King for being too myopic. He tells his audience that "not long after talking about that dream I started seeing it turn into a nightmare" (257). King came to see, as Cone teaches his readers, what Malcolm X had seen all along: innocent African Americans murdered by white racists, African Americans suffering in poverty in a wealthy society, African Americans rioting out of frustration at the slow pace of the movement, Americans in general dying for an unjust cause in Vietnam.

The King that emerges in 1967 is a King chastened by the failure of American democracy. Still, as he tells his auditors at the end of the sermon, he has a dream, but it is a dream more global, more Edenic than the dream of 1963 (257–58).

Globally, King envisions a world where humans realize "that they are made to live together" as siblings. He speaks now not only of Americans but of Chinese, Russians, Africans, in short, all people of the world. This 1967 King, rooted in America as a black Baptist preacher, moves beyond America, beyond the pan-African dreams of Du Bois and even the pan-people of color dreams of Malcolm X, into a global vision of the human communion.

Yet, he doesn't lose sight of the particular problems of "Negroes" and "every colored person in the world" (258). While King is certainly concerned about all peoples of all races, he offers a prime place to people of color. His global vision does not hide the particular difficulties that people of color face. Still, even this concern for people of color is globalized. In the "I Have a Dream" speech, King dreamed of time when his "four little children will one day live in a nation where they will not be judged by the color of their skin but by the content of their character" (219). Here, in this sermon, this line becomes globalized. He dreams of a world where each person of color "will be judged on the basis of the content of his character rather than the color of his skin."

So too, King dreams of a warless globe, no doubt a dream that arises in the context of both the Cold War and the raging hot war in Vietnam. The dreams of "I Have a Dream" were entirely concerned about the Civil Rights movement in America. This sermon, representing King's shift toward Malcolm X's perspective, moves beyond the "integrated cup of coffee" into the pressing issues of wars over land. Utopically, with a hint of his desire for the garden, King dreams of "that one day" when "war will come to an end," when "men will beat their swords into plowshares and their spears into pruning hooks" (258). It is not insignificant that King alludes here to the biblical dream of tools of destruction being transformed into tools of the garden. The divisiveness of the Fall, manifest in wars over land fought with terrible weapons, is healed in this dream. Weapons become implements. The land becomes a site of care and concern rather than a site of battle and death.

This vision leads to the final, Edenic climax of the sermon:

> I still have a dream today that one day the lamb and the lion will lie down together and every man will sit under his own vine and fig tree and none shall be afraid. I still have a dream today that one day every valley shall be exalted and every mountain and hill will be made low, the rough places will be made smooth and the crooked places straight, and the glory of the Lord shall be revealed, and all flesh shall see it together. . . . It will be a glorious day, the morning stars will sing together, and the sons of God will shout for joy. (258)

King's Edenic desire could not be more obvious, and its location could not be less obvious. Unlike the 1963 "I Have a Dream" speech, which clearly composes Eden with reference to the American landscape and sociopolitical situation, this Edenic vision is placeless. This lack of specificity is only appropriate, given King's intense global commitment at the end of his life. If he had composed Eden here with American landmarks, he would have belied his own message that humans live within an "inescapable network of mutuality" (254). As King moved into the world, his dream of Eden followed. Unlike Du Bois, who left America for Africa, King leaves America for nowhere, for everywhere, for a dream of Eden beyond parochial times and spaces.

Here, in this Eden unspecified, harmony abounds. The natural realm is itself healed, with antagonists like the lamb and lion transformed into companions, even comrades, sharing space peacefully, without rancor, bloodshed, death. So too, humans, having beat their swords into plowshares, their spears into pruning hooks, having, in short, become gardeners, find themselves at home in the natural order. No longer battling over land, no longer afraid, they rest under vines and figs.

Borrowing from "I Have a Dream," King again introduces into this harmonious scene the presence of God. Whereas Du Bois envisioned his Eden as nearly godless, King, ever the preacher, invokes the glory of the Lord. The lamb and lion experience God like the inhabitants of the originary garden.

The sermon ends with a rapturous sentence, again presenting King's belief that all life-forms interpenetrate each other. Humans and the stars themselves cry joyfully with the realization that the garden has come again, with the knowledge that the Fall has ended, that the legend of Eden has become more than hearsay, more than the stories of old.

6 | Conclusion

> Only revolutionary movements seem to offer an
> appropriate stage for the exercise of the power of
> speaking.
>
> —Julia Kristeva, *Language the Unknown*

Unfolded in the previous chapters is this, essentially: emancipatory composition, oral and written, rooted in the play of theological and political tropes, is a two-part practice. First, the emancipatory composer—be he or she a professional or a first-year student—must know the language of the dominant culture. Second, the composer must embrace what Kenneth Burke calls "the comic attitude."

As Patricia Bizzell suggests, the acquisition of a culture's vocabulary was central to classical education: "The classical curriculum prescribes readings in history, literature, and philosophy for the rhetorician-in-training. Quintilian, for example, goes so far as to name specific authors who should be read" (2). For our own time, an exegesis of the works of Du Bois, King, and Malcolm X suggest that theological and political tropes are, in particular, central to this prescription. Second, the composer—be he or she a professional or a first-year student—must be able to find within this language contradictory, oppositional, subversive connotations. It is not enough to recite the received language if emancipation is the aim. Rather, the received language must be turned over, around, inside-out.

Strangely, this book's elucidation of what it calls "emancipatory composition"—with its emphasis on the centrality of the acquisition and reformation of theological and political tropes central to the American experience—places it in friendly conversation with E. D. Hirsch and his infamous idea: "cultural literacy." It is strange because the "cultural Right" that has strongly championed Hirsch would find various aspects of Du Bois's, King's, and Malcolm X's theopolitical compositional practices problematic.

The Right, exemplified by Dr. William Bennett, the former Reagan administration education secretary who champions Hirsch's work (*Cultural Literacy* vii, xiv), and by leaders of the Exxon Education Foundation who encouraged Hirsch to write *Cultural Literacy*, finds in the idea of cultural literacy the salvation of America. However, the Right might not find Du Bois's discovery of Eden in Africa, Malcolm X's strong condemnation of American racism, and King's riposte against American involvement in Vietnam to its liking.

Even stranger is this: Hirsch, and the phrase he represents, has been much maligned by the "cultural Left." The same Left that might champion the works of Du Bois, King, and Malcolm X might take umbrage at any reading of these heroes of progressive compositional practice that does not place them in opposition to Hirsch. They understand *Cultural Literacy*, and even "cultural literacy," to be hopelessly retrograde, reactionary, perhaps even a bit fascistic. As far as the Left is concerned, *Cultural Literacy* cannot, simply cannot, help the cause of emancipation, cannot serve emancipatory composition.

Consider, for instance, Barbara Hernstein Smith ("Cult-Lit"), Henry Giroux ("Liberal Arts"), Leila Christenbury ("Cultural"), and Ray Browne and Arthur Neal ("Many Tongues"). Smith, Christenbury, and Brown and Neal all share one criticism of the idea of cultural literacy in general, and Hirsch's work in particular. They think, in Smith's words, that there is no "macroculture" that can offer a "transcendent" literacy. For these four, all literacies are parochial, bound to particular communities. At one level, they are correct. The dimension of literacy that a professor of composition has as an academic is certainly different from the literacy that an electrician has. The electrician can understand, for instance, complicated network designs and instructions that the professor might only be able to look at with the sense that, yes, that page contains writing. However, these theorists seem to have purchased the whole of contemporary relativism without a discerning eye. While the electrician and the professor have different professional literacies, they do share elements of a cultural literacy. As Hirsch would say, they would both be able to recognize, within a web of shared allusions, phrases like "the American flag" or "the Declaration of Independence."

Smith might grant this but claim, as she does, that even if the electrician and the professor share a cultural literacy at the level of words, it is highly unlikely that they share the same associations those words represent. This is Smith's strongest point, and it is echoed by and made more sharply by Giroux. As he says, the idea of cultural literacy, at least Hirsch's idea, presumes that literacy and culture do not participate in struggles over power.

The most conservative understanding of the acquisition of cultural archives might assume that one should acquire cultural knowledge without calling that knowledge into question. This, without doubt, is at the heart of Paulo Freire's distinction between "banking" and "liberatory" education. Banking presumes that the acquisition of cultural knowledge should, and does, occur without question, without challenge.

With Freire and many others, I suggest that literacy and culture are at once given and the result of the "dynamics of struggle and power." Americans, for instance, are born into a cultural literacy. The word "capitalism," to take one, is part of their birthright, their originary language. The problem arises when society, represented by schools, newspapers, political leaders, tries to mask the fact that the word "capitalism" is fraught with ambiguity, that it is a site of struggle.

Browne and Neal's essay is, finally, ironically contradictory. They argue for a conception of literacy based more on contemporary life and contemporary modes of communication than on history and print media, but their essay is full of the historical, culturally literate, conservative allusions that Hirsch champions as central to a functioning American democracy (for example, Thomas Jefferson and "Judeo-Christian culture" on 158, "Babel" on 167, Alexander Pope on 169, "Ben Franklin's Boston" on 170). One cannot read their essay with complete fruitfulness unless one knows these terms or is willing to learn them.

The stakes in the struggle over cultural literacy are high, much higher than standard academic debates in the humanities. Cultural literacy concerns not merely academics who tweak each other in refereed journals. Rather, it concerns all Americans. As Bizzell notes, the idea of cultural literacy, or cultural archives, dates at least to Quintilian. Part of the debate over cultural literacy is a debate over the continuity of culture and whether there is, in fact, "culture" or just heterogeneous cultures that happen to coexist in the same geographical or national space. Bizzell argues quite rightly that America comprises heterogeneous cultures, or discourse communities, that nonetheless comprise what might be called American culture (4–5).

Of course, cultural literacy is not simply about the acquisition of knowledge, as Hirsch tends to argue. Rather, it is also about what one does with this knowledge. Bizzell holds rightly that compositionists have become trapped in the "false dichotomy of knowing and doing" (1). The "process" movement in writing has tended to emphasize the doing to the exclusion of the knowing. Yet, teachers of composition are also cautioned, even as they begin to embrace the "knowing" part of the equation, not to forget the doing.

This touches on what is, perhaps, Hirsch's greatest problem. While he is quite correct to argue that there is a vocabulary central to the American experience, a vocabulary we would all do well to share, Hirsch mistakenly suggests that there is no doing to be done with these things that should be known. In his discussion of what he calls the national vocabulary, Hirsch maintains that this vocabulary "is primarily an instrument of communication among diverse cultures rather than a cultural or class instrument in its own right" (104). As my reading of Du Bois, King, and Malcolm X shows, the national vocabulary—represented by the four tropes that are at the center of the book—does serve as an instrument of communication among diverse cultures. As Bizzell has argued, it is what allows the oppressed to speak to the oppressor in ways the oppressor can understand.

However, Hirsch's view on the nature of cultural literacy is limited. The vocabulary is a means of communication, but not only that. It is, as a reading of Du Bois, King, and Malcolm illustrates, a cultural and class instrument as well. Remember, for instance, Du Bois's concentration of the capitalization of certain words, King's concentration on "black," Malcolm X's concentration on the phrase "human rights." Each understood that vocabulary itself is a tool of power and that power is wielded, dispersed, challenged, through vocabulary.

The second part of emancipatory composition involves, then, what the American rhetorical theorist Kenneth Burke has called the "comic attitude" (*Attitudes* 173, 344). In short, the comic attitude is aware of and exploits the heterogeneity of language. Burke, for instance, argues that those who would promote peace would do well to look at the rhetoric of war because the rhetoric of war contains within itself the seeds of its own subversion (*Philosophy* 238). The comic attitude allows one to discover within discourse the suppressed other, the hidden opposite, the "up" in "down," the "in" of "out," the "man" in "woman," the "peace" in "war."

An astute reading of Du Bois, King, and Malcolm X—which this book purports to offer—discovers this comic attitude at work. Each accepts the familiar language of the community only to transform it. Each is at once conservative, a composer whose words often arise from the deepest sedimentary layers of America's theological and political psyche. At the same time, each is an extremist. Each uses America's cultural vocabulary, its tropes, in order to emancipate the oppressed and oppressors alike.

Three dimensions of the Fall that Kenneth Burke identifies as central to that trope inform the rhetorics of Du Bois, King, and Malcolm X—violence, socioeconomic division, and Babel. Each dimension serves to describe the situation of the color line in America, teaching us that the Fall involves race. The Orient, with its three connotations—the yellow, alien other, the wise person, and a backward place—serves both as an ally of African Americans and as a critic of the West. For its part, Africa and its typical American meanings—Africa as a site of suffering and Africa as monstrous/noble—help Du Bois, King, and Malcolm X criticize the West and reimage African Americans. Finally, Eden—with the standard American hope that paradise is rooted in the American landscape—allows these three to move beyond the American possibility into other spaces more hospitable. Each finally looks beyond even an American democracy come to full fruition as a Ciceronian republic. Du Bois, King, and Malcolm X draw on the webs of meaning provided by Eden in order to move beyond American democracy, in order to rend asunder the culture that provides them with the words that inform their work. They are conservative. They are extremists. They are radicals.

This, finally, is the challenge of any who would practice emancipatory composition: embrace the theological and political language that is the American birthright and turn it up, down, around. Be conservative. Be extreme. Be radical.

Notes
Works Cited
Index

Notes

1 | Emancipatory Composition

1. At Indiana University East, I taught the *Autobiography* to a class that was composed of Caucasian females, entirely. These were rural or small-town women who had had little experience with African American life and little knowledge of the problems with which urban folk struggle. To a woman, they found the book to be fascinating, the struggle of Malcolm Little/Detroit Red/Satan/Minister Malcolm X to be riveting. Their response speaks well of them, of the American educational system that prepared them to read this book, of the culture industry that, no doubt, prepared them to accept the actual words of Malcolm X (and those of Alex Haley, of course) by inundating them with Malcolm X's image.

    Of course, my students' easy and welcoming reception of Malcolm X may be more problematic than my initial interpretation suggests. Rather than an indication of the wonderful, open plurality of which American democracy is capable, it may indicate that the American culture industry has again tamed a potentially revolutionary metaphor in order to appease uneasy citizens and in order to make money. As Dyson suggests in *Making Malcolm*, "Malcolm's cultural renaissance—his improbable second coming—brims with irony" (xiii). After all, my students were the target of Malcolm X's anti-Caucasian rhetoric. They were, in his mind at one of his stages, devils. In another of his stages, they were a devilish experiment gone awry, genetic mutations resulting from the play of an evil genius. That my students were able to embrace the power of Malcolm X's life is, indeed, ironic.

2. Handy offers a fine book-length treatment of this issue, demonstrating conclusively the ways in which the sociopolitical and the religious are woven together in American discourse.

2 | The Fall

1. I have discussed this elsewhere. See Stull 52.
2. The Conference on College Composition and Communication weighed in on the dialect issue in the early 1970s. See the special fall 1974 issue of *College Composition and Communication* to read the resolution titled "The Students' Right to Their Own Language." This resolution supports the validity of dialects.
3. See Taylor for a fine treatment of Du Bois's struggle over definition. Taylor argues that Du Bois offers this definition of African Americans: "[B]lacks were innocent victims of white society, possessors of a superior soul, uniquely beautiful, and blood brothers of the majority of mankind. Finally, and most profoundly, they were men" (187). This is a sound reading of Du Bois, though not particularly crucial to my argument. My point, finally, is that Du Bois was aware of the linguistic plurality (the Babel) of American discourse, especially as it reveals itself in the definition of terms, and that this letter to Wilson well manifests Du Bois's awareness.

   Taylor also argues that Du Bois used numerous strategies to contest definitions, among them logical analysis, statistics, and countertestimony. Du Bois's suggestion to Wilson, that he come to know some African Americans personally, might fall under Taylor's category of countertestimony. It also, and this would be a fascinating line to pursue, could be thought of in terms of empiricism, which Du Bois learned from James at Harvard. Du Bois is finally suggesting that Wilson personally *experience* the meaning of the term rather than rely on the language of others. This, as I have said in the main text of the essay, includes Du Bois himself. He does not say to Wilson, "Take my word for it." He says, in effect, "Find out for yourself." See Byerman's dissertation for one elucidation of this idea. He finds in Du Bois a "tension between an empiricist mode of perception and an idealist system of morality" (v).
4. Byerman offers a Lacanian reading of Du Bois, emphasizing, as such a reading must, the place of language in Du Bois's work. Byerman concentrates on Du Bois's sociology and fiction. Byerman's thesis only supports my own point here, though I have not approached Du Bois from a psychoanalytic vantage:

   > Du Bois presents to us subtextually an endless struggle of power and oppression, father and son, black and white in both racial

and moral senses. It is a struggle not only for social justice, but for control over language. . . . He would seize the word, so as to name the world. (*Seizing* 8; see also 201)

Byerman, like Taylor, also discusses Du Bois's struggle with definition. For Byerman, "race" is a key term in Du Bois's work. As Byerman understands it, Du Bois struggles with the meaning of the word in order to "overthrow the discursive control of the dominant culture." To do so, Byerman argues, Du Bois operated within an "Eurocentric ideological framework" (*Seizing* 81–84). This is similar to the point I am making: Du Bois, King, and Malcolm X borrow elements of the American rhetorical heritage in order to subvert it.

5. See my *Religious Dialectics of Pain and Imagination* for a discussion of Freire's counterreading of the place of Portuguese. As I argue, Freire is convinced that Portuguese is the linguistic tool of an oppressive colonial system. Freire believed that emerging nations of color, like Guinea-Bissau, should have embraced a more indigenous language, such as Creole. Portuguese, Freire argues, only propagates white European imperial and colonial attitudes and images. Du Bois, no doubt, was flush with antagonism toward the "Anglo-Saxon idea" (*Selections* 1: 181).

6. See Arndt for a discussion of two important themes in Du Bois's editorials, especially those of the years 1919–1929: the Negro as citizen of the world and the Negro as citizen of the U.S. Du Bois, like many who are alienated from the American republic, refused (until his move to Ghana at the end of his life) to dissociate himself completely from his birth-country. Nonetheless, he found its resources finally incapable of providing the critique necessary to engender social justice for African Americans.

7. Many have argued that Du Bois most wanted to influence the elite. As Rudwick maintains, the *Crisis* was "produced for an educated Negro public" (152).

8. Keele claims that "the strategy of definition was the primary rhetorical basis from which Dr. King attempted to persuade his auditors" (148). Keele's claim is overstated, however. As subsequent studies of King convincingly demonstrate, his rhetoric was not primarily "about" definition. Keith Miller and Lischer, for instance, discuss the idea, albeit differently, that King's persuasive power came from his ability to weave together the African American oral tradition and the European American literate tradition.

9. Malcolm X's use of the term "man" is problematic. See Cone for an

outstanding discussion of the place of gender in King's and Malcolm X's works and lives.

10. Cornel West, critiquing Malcolm X on this point, claims that this metaphor is a fine "rhetorical device" but "fails as a persuasive description." He asserts that many middle-class African Americans have a field-Negro mentality and many poor African Americans have a house-Negro mentality ("Malcolm X" 50–51). However, West's criticism also buttresses Malcolm X's basic point: African Americans are divided from other African Americans by property, and this property division is intimately linked with the color line.

3 | The Orient

1. Oddly, Lischer claims that "for a brief period in his career [King] exegeted love as Gandhian *satyagraha*" but that "Gandhi was foreign to King's own religious heritage and positively unintelligible to his America audience. By 1960 references to Gandhi disappeared from King's sermons and speeches" (214). This is an odd claim for at least three reasons.

First, the claim that Gandhi disappeared from King's sermons and speeches by 1960 is simply not true. In the 1962 speech "The Ethical Demands for Integration," King claims that "The Gandhian concept of noninjury parallels the Hebraic-Christian teaching of the sacredness of every human being" (124).

Second, Lischer's claim that allusions to Gandhi were unintelligible to King's audience is simply assertion and defies King's own testimony. Lischer does not offer any audience analysis, even post-facto analysis, as it must be at this point. How does he know it was unintelligible? Also, King himself saw Gandhi as intelligible. In "An Experiment in Love," King relates that Gandhi was on everybody's lips during the Montgomery bus boycott (17). King also suggests, in "The Time for Freedom Has Come," that the student sit-in protesters identified with Gandhi (164).

Third, the "foreignness" of Gandhi is precisely King's point. Like Du Bois and Malcolm X, King sought connections outside of America strictly defined as such. Gandhi, for King, was part of the African America landscape because he provided the method for the spirit of Jesus Christ ("Pilgrimage to Nonviolence" 38).

2. As Keith Miller argues, King learned Gandhi indirectly and redacted Gandhi to suit his own purposes (88–99). Miller persuasively argues that King's Gandhi is the Gandhi he learned from a circle of Howard University–related, African American intellectuals. King's contribution was that he "grafted Gandhian principles onto the worldview of African-American Protestants" (96). While keeping the notions of *satyagraha* and nonviolent resistance, King, Miller reminds his readers, "ignored many of Gandhi's most fundamental religious values and practices" (99). These include vegetarianism, sexual abstinence, a weekly day of silence, advocacy of home industry, and, most dramatically, the use of the hunger strike.

3. See Rampersand and Byerman (*Seizing*) for outstanding, and very different, discussions of Du Bois as a man of letters. Rampersand presents a humanistic overview of Du Bois's life and work. Byerman offers a Lacanian reading of Du Bois. Both, however, remind Du Bois scholars that he was, above all, an intellectual wordsmith. It seems to me that, finally, this is what separates Du Bois from King. King, as Keith Miller and Lischer persuasively argue, was ever the preacher, even though he held a Ph.D. in systematic theology from Boston University. Du Bois, however, was fundamentally an intellectual man of letters.

4. For discussions of Du Bois's relationship to Christianity, see, for instance, Rudwick 155–56; Marable 31; Rampersand 19 and 41.

4 | Africa

1. Surprisingly, however, given his training, expertise, and interest in the rhetorical construction of reality, King did not engage in a similar analytic venture. This is despite the fact that he was theoretically attuned to the importance of discourse. His treatment of the word "black" reveals that King was able to engage not only the somatic reality of African Americans suffering under an unjust system; he was, as well, able to engage language as an object in need of critique.

It is impossible to determine why King, unlike Du Bois, did not analyze "Africanist discourse." It is not as if he was not interested in Africa. It is not as if Africa, as I will discuss later in this chapter, was not allusively and powerfully present throughout his work. For whatever reasons, King simply did not engage Africanist discourse as an object in need of critique. He produced discourse about Africa, but he did not, as a part of this production, analyze it too.

2. Reminiscent of his claim regarding the place of Gandhi in King's work, Lischer maintains that although "in late career he [King] began mentioning Africa and substituting names of black artists and thinkers for the 'greats' of earlier sermons," Africa in general and Ethiopia in particular were relatively unimportant for King (216). As I will discuss in this chapter, Africa is, in fact, pervasively present in King's work.

   Moreover, and strangely so, Lischer himself indicates the interpenetrative play of Africa and King. First, as Lischer claims, the "*nommo*"—the "creative spoken word of Africa"—was central to Ebenezer Baptist Church rhetoric and thus central to King's rhetoric (22). While one might wonder to which "Africa" Lischer refers (for instance, is *nommo* true of the entire continent?), his point is well taken. Thus, even if one were to grant Lischer his argument that Africa in general and Ethiopia in particular were relatively unimportant in King's work as "words," Lischer himself argues that "Africa" (whatever that might mean) is central to King's work. Indeed, he suggests that "the rhythms of the epic" that arose out of Africa "engulfed the hearer into an exquisite partnership with the poet" and were central to King's rhetorical performances (120).

   Too, Lischer provides a fascinating and important discussion of an early King sermon, "The Birth of a New Nation," that King used to celebrate the independence of Ghana and analogously call for the freedom of African Americans (Lischer 203–4). While it is true that King did not again offer such a detailed and lengthy analogical exploration of Africa and America, Africa does not disappear from King's work only to reappear "in late career." It is surprising that Lischer's fine study of this sermon did not alert him to the ways in which King continued to compose Africa.

3. See Cone for a brief discussion of Malcolm X's treatment of the Congo relative to the voting rights drive in the South. Cone tells of the time Malcolm X delivered a speech at a voting rights rally in Selma, Alabama, upon the invitation of the Student Nonviolent Coordinating Committee (SNCC). King was in jail, and Malcolm X was warned by leaders Andrew Young and James Bevel to focus on voting rights. Malcolm X ignored them and linked the voting rights drive to the actions of the American government in the Congo. Ap-

parently "both blacks and whites raised questions about the relevance of his internationalist perspective for the right of blacks to go to the polls in Dallas County. But for Malcolm the two issues were the same" (210).

As Cone goes on to write, "Malcolm viewed himself as a warrior against worldwide white supremacy" (210). While some, in terms of cultural literacy, might read "Selma" and "voting rights" with strictly domestic meaning, Malcolm X followed their allusive webs to other sites around the world. While some might read "Congo" with strictly foreign meaning, Malcolm X followed its allusive web back home to America.

4. See Lewis for an excellent discussion of the pageant. As he argues:

> "The Star of Ethiopia" was the most patent, expansive use yet made by Du Bois of an ideology of black supremacy in order to confound one of white supremacy. In its fabulous dramaturgy, he worked out the basics of an Afrocentric aesthetics and historiography. (461)

5 | Eden

1. For a more detailed discussion of Merton's treatment of Eden, see my *Religious Dialectics of Pain and Imagination* 62–66. As I argue there, Merton himself thinks that search for a paradisiacal place is foolhardy, always impossible, always tainted by the desire to pillage paradise. In the words of an old Joni Mitchell song, humans "pave paradise to put up a parking lot."

2. McDowell, star of such films as *Green Card*; *Sex, Lies, and Videotape*; and *Groundhog Day*, met her husband before she began her acting career. Both were models, hired by The Gap clothing company to pose for an advertisement. The Gap, as many readers may know, caters to a young, upscale clientele seeking casual clothing that is, at once, "classic" and "mod." That McDowell and Qualley met as models on a Gap advertisement project and now own a little piece of heaven on earth is stunningly appropriate for a magazine directed to readers who, one must presume, love wealthy, beautiful people who are able to buy paradise.

3. Rampersand also locates Du Bois's adult activity in his Massachu-

setts childhood. While Rampersand does not emphasize the Edenic quality of Du Bois's rememberings, he does maintain that "the ordered life and simple beauty of the small New England town remained for a long time Du Bois's model of civic polity" (7).

4. Sadly, perhaps, it is not the report of a mystical experience. It becomes clear in the September 1913 piece titled "The Great Northwest" that this phrase refers, literally, to a sailing trip. In the September piece, Du Bois refines his memory: "There came an interlude—a perfect day on perfect waters, flying northward where hurry the shadow of undropped snows and the peace of endless understanding. For that one day of rest I thank thee, Perfect Spirit" (*Selections* 1: 68).

5. See, for instance, Cone 58–88, Ansbro 187–93, Keele 156–87, Calloway-Thomas and Lucaites 9, Lucaites and Condit 93–94, Walton 5–7, 69–70, and Donald Hugh Smith 239. Cone, by far, offers the most brilliant discussion of King's dream. What he fails to see, however, is the Edenic quality of King's vision that Keith Miller has begun to discern. Ansbro offers a lucid discussion of the "beloved community" in King's work, offering particular insight into how "agape" plays out in this vision. Yet Ansbro, as well, fails to see the post-historical, Edenic quality in the dream.

Keele, for her part, attempts to read King's dream as thoroughly American, not daring, finally, to step beyond the American cultural tradition. Keele fails to see that King, in fact, was radically critical of America, that he did move beyond a simple allegiance to the "American Dream," that he did foresee the end of history and thus America itself. See Cone for a fine discussion of King's disenchantment with America (213–43).

Calloway-Thomas and Lucaites and Lucaites and Condit helpfully argue that the "beloved community" is a rhetorical construct, pointing to the essential fact about King: he was a rhetorician.

Walton, along with everyone else who has written on the "beloved community," claims that it guided King's work. He also claims, oddly, that King never defines it. One must grant that King does not offer a single line that says "The beloved community is . . . ," but certainly its characteristics, as I will argue, are clear. As Keith Miller says, King essentially invokes the Edenic desires of Isaiah: the landscape of the world is transformed, made holy enough for humans to see God, as they did in the garden.

It would be interesting to hear an extended conversation between

Walton and Ansbro. Ansbro claims that King's vision is finally rooted in God. Walton, in contrast, holds that King's vision arose from the founding documents of the American republic. This dynamic points to an interesting "problem" with King: to whom does he belong—theopolitical activists or just political activists? Hirsch, it must be noted, never deals with the ramifications of King's theopolitical status. King spoke, after all, as an American Christian minister, not simply as an American.

Smith, with a helpful quantitative claim, offers this to the conversation: the "beloved community" is the third most frequent trope in King's work.

Works Cited

Adorno, Theodor W. *Aesthetic Theory.* Trans. C. Lenhardt. Ed. Gretel Adorno and Rolf Tiedemann. London: Routledge, 1984.

Allende, Isabel. *The Infinite Plan.* New York: HarperCollins, 1991.

Ansbro, John J. *Martin Luther King, Jr.: The Making of a Mind.* Maryknoll, NY: Orbis, 1982.

Arndt, Murray Dennis. "The Crisis Years of W. E. B. Du Bois, 1910–1934." Diss. Duke U, 1970.

Berry, Wendell. *The Hidden Wound.* San Francisco: North Point, 1989.

Bizzell, Patricia. "The Function of Cultural Archives in Persuasion: The Examples of Frederick Douglass and William Apess." CCCC Convention. Milwaukee, 1996.

Bloch, Ernst. *The Principle of Hope.* Trans. Neville Plaice, Stephen Plaice, and Paul Knight. 2 vols. Cambridge: MIT P, 1986.

Broderick, Francis L. *W. E. B. Du Bois: Negro Leader in a Time of Crisis.* Stanford: Stanford UP, 1959.

Browne, Ray B., and Arthur G. Neal. "The Many Tongues of Literacy." *Journal of Popular Culture* 25 (1): 157–86.

Burke, Kenneth. *Attitudes Toward History.* 3rd ed. Berkeley: U of California P, 1984.

———. *The Philosophy of Literary Form.* Berkeley: U of California P, 1973.

———. *A Rhetoric of Motives.* Berkeley: U of California P, 1969.

Byerman, Keith E. *Seizing the Word: History, Art, and Self in the Work of W. E. B. Du Bois.* Athens: U of Georgia P, 1994.

———. "Two Warring Ideals: The Dialectical Thought of W. E. B. Du Bois." Diss. Purdue U, 1978.

Calloway-Thomas, Carolyn, and John Louis Lucaites, eds. *Martin Luther King, Jr., and the Sermonic Power of Public Discourse.* Tuscaloosa: U of Alabama P, 1993.

Christenbury, Leila. "Cultural Literacy: A Terrible Idea Whose Time Has Come." *English Journal* 78 (1): 14–17.

Condit, Celeste Michelle, and John Lucaites. *Crafting Equality: America's Anglo-African Word.* Chicago: U of Chicago P, 1993.

Cone, James. *Malcolm and Martin and America: A Dream or a Nightmare.* Maryknoll, NY: Orbis, 1991.

Covino, William A., and David A. Jolliffe. *Rhetoric: Concepts, Definitions, Boundaries.* Boston: Allyn, 1995.

Do the Right Thing. Dir. Spike Lee. With Danny Aiello, Ossie Davis, Ruby Lee, Richard Edson, Giancarlo Esposito, Spike Lee, Bill Nunn, John Turturro. 40 Acres and a Mule, 1989.

Du Bois, W. E. B. *The Autobiography of W. E. B. Du Bois: A Soliloquy on Viewing My Life from the Last Decade of Its First Century.* Stone Mountain, GA: International, 1968.

———. *Selections from* The Crisis. Comp. and ed. Herbert Aptheker. 2 vols. Millwood, NY: Kraus-Thomson, 1983.

Dyson, Michael Eric. *Making Malcolm: The Myth and Meaning of Malcolm X.* New York: Oxford UP, 1995.

Fell, Mary. *The Persistence of Memory.* New York: Random, 1984.

Ford, Lynn. "Upward March." *Indianapolis Star* 14 Oct. 1995: E1+.

Freire, Paulo. *Pedagogy of the Oppressed.* New York: Seabury, 1974.

Freire, Paulo, and Donaldo Macedo. *Literacy: Reading the Word and the World.* South Hadley, MA: Bergin, 1987.

Gilroy, Paul. *The Black Atlantic: Modernity and Double Consciousness.* Cambridge: Harvard UP, 1993.

Giroux, Henry. "Liberal Arts Education and the Struggle for Public Life: Dreaming about Democracy." *South Atlantic Quarterly* 89 (1): 114–38.

———. *Schooling and the Struggle for Public Life.* Minneapolis: U of Minnesota P, 1988.

———. *Teachers as Intellectuals: Toward a Critical Pedagogy of Learning.* Granby, MA: Bergin, 1988.

Golden, Renny, and Michael McConnell. *Sanctuary: The New Underground Railroad.* Maryknoll, NY: Orbis, 1986.

Handy, Robert T. *A Christian America: Protestant Hopes and Historical Realities.* 2nd ed. New York: Oxford UP, 1984.

Hirsch, E. D., Jr. *Cultural Literacy: What Every American Needs to Know.* New York: Vintage, 1988.

———. *The Philosophy of Composition.* Chicago: U of Chicago P, 1977.

Hutchins, David. "A Little Piece of Heaven." *InStyle* August 1995: 5, 60–69.

Karim, Benjamin. Introduction. *The End of White World Supremacy: Four Speeches.* By Malcolm X. Ed. Benjamin Karim. New York: Arcade, 1971. 1–22.

Keele, Lucy Anne McCandish. "A Burkeian Analysis of the Rhetorical Strategies of Dr. Martin Luther King, Jr., 1955–1968." Diss. U of Oregon, 1972.

King, Martin Luther, Jr. *A Testament of Hope: The Essential Writings and Speeches of Martin Luther King, Jr.* Ed. James M. Washington. San Francisco: HarperSanFrancisco, 1991.

Kozol, Jonathan. *Illiterate America.* New York: Anchor, 1985.

Kristeva, Julia. *Language the Unknown: An Initiation into Linguistics.* Trans. Anne M. Menke. New York: Columbia UP, 1989.

Legends of the Fall. Dir. Edward Zwick. With Brad Pitt, Anthony Hopkins, and Aidan Quinn. Columbia Tristar, 1995.

Lewis, David Levering. *W. E. B. Du Bois: Biography of a Race 1868–1919.* New York: Henry Holt, 1993.

Lischer, Richard. *The Preacher King: Martin Luther King, Jr. and the Word That Moved America.* New York: Oxford UP, 1995.

Lucaites, John Louis, and Celeste Michelle Condit. "Universalizing 'Equality': The Public Legacy of Martin Luther King, Jr." *Martin Luther King, Jr., and the Sermonic Power of Public Discourse.* Ed. Carolyn Calloway-Thomas and John Louis Lucaites. Tuscaloosa: U of Alabama P, 1993. 85–103, 196 n. 4.

Malcolm X. *The Autobiography of Malcolm X.* New York: Ballantine, 1964.

———. *By Any Means Necessary.* New York: Pathfinder, 1970.

———. *The End of White World Supremacy: Four Speeches.* New York: Arcade, 1971.

———. *February 1965: The Final Speeches.* New York: Pathfinder, 1992.

———. *The Last Speeches of Malcolm X.* Ed. Bruce Perry. New York: Pathfinder, 1989.

———. *Malcolm X Speaks: Selected Speeches and Statements.* Ed. George Breitman. New York: Grove Weidenfeld, 1965.

———. *Malcolm X Talks to Young People: Speeches in the U.S., Britain, and Canada.* New York: Pathfinder, 1965.

Marable, Manning. *W. E. B. Du Bois: Black Radical Democrat.* Boston: Twayne, 1986.

Merton, Thomas. "From Pilgrimage to Crusade." *Mystics and Zen Masters.* New York: Farrar, 1967. 91–112.

Miller, Christopher L. *Blank Darkness: Africanist Discourse in French.* Chicago: U of Chicago P, 1985.

Miller, Keith. *Voice of Deliverance: The Language of Martin Luther King, Jr., and Its Sources.* New York: Free, 1992.

The Next Karate Kid. Dir. Christopher Cain. With Pat Morita and Hilary Swank. Columbia Tristar, 1994.

Niebuhr, Reinhold. *An Interpretation of Christian Ethics.* New York: Seabury, 1935.

Ogden, Schubert M. *Faith and Freedom: Toward a Theology of Liberation.* Nashville: Abingdon, 1979.

Rampersand, Arnold. *The Art and Imagination of W. E. B. Du Bois.* Cambridge: Harvard UP, 1976.

Rorty, Richard. *Contingency, irony, and solidarity.* Cambridge: Cambridge UP, 1989.

Rudwick, Elliot. *Propagandist of the Negro Protest.* 2nd ed. Philadelphia: U of Pennsylvania P, 1968.

Said, Edward. *Orientalism.* New York: Pantheon, 1978.

School Daze. Dir. Spike Lee. With Julian Eaves, Jane Troussaint, Tisha Campbell, and Laurence Fishburne. 40 Acres and a Mule, 1987.

Smith, Barbara Hernstein. "Cult-Lit: Hirsch, Literacy, and the 'National Culture.' " *South Atlantic Quarterly* 89 (1): 69–88.

Smith, Donald Hugh. "Martin Luther King, Jr.: Rhetorician of Revolt." Diss. U of Wisconsin, 1964.

Staples, Brent. "Just Walk on by: A Black Man Ponders His Power to Alter Public Space." *Developing Connections: A Writer's Guide with Readings.* Ed. Judith A. Stanford. Mountain View, CA: Mayfield, 1995. 244–48.

Stull, Bradford T. *Religious Dialectics of Pain and Imagination.* Albany: State U of New York P, 1994.

Taylor, Carol McDonald. "W. E. B. Du Bois: The Rhetoric of Redefinition." Diss. U of Oregon, 1971.

Walton, Hanes, Jr. *The Political Philosophy of Martin Luther King, Jr.* Westport, CT: Greenwood, 1971.

West, Cornel. "Malcolm X and Black Rage." *Malcolm X: In Our Own Image.* Ed. Joe Wood. New York: St. Martin's, 1992. 48–58.

———. *Race Matters.* Boston: Beacon, 1993.

Index

Bradford T. Stull is an assistant professor of English and communications at Rivier College. The author of *Religious Dialectics of Pain and Imagination,* he was educated at Phillips University, the University of Chicago, and the University of Illinois at Chicago.